TOK

Diaspora Dialogues
presents

TOK

book 3
Helen Walsh, editor

Zephyr Press

Zephyr Press
170 Bloor Street West, Suite 804
Toronto, Ontario M5S 1T9
www.zephyrpress.ca

Library and Archives Canada Cataloguing in Publication

   Tok : diaspora dialogues / Helen Walsh, editor.

ISBN 978-0-9734112-5-6

   1. Short stories, Canadian (English)—Ontario—Toronto.
2. Canadian poetry (English)—Ontario—Toronto.
3. Canadian fiction (English)—21st century.
4. Toronto (Ont.)—Literary collections. I. Walsh, Helen, 1965–

PS8237.T6T54 2006   C810.8'032713541   C2006-902670-X

Book design and composition by The Office of Gilbert Li
Copyediting by Madeline Koch
Cover painting by Keli Maksud
Printed and bound in Canada by Transcontinental Inc.

The paper used in this book contains 100% post-consumer fibre,
is acid-free, processed chlorine free, EcoLogo-certified, and was
manufactured with biogas energy.

Racial profiling. The difficulties and humour in cross-cultural communication. Being young, urban, hip and in love. The alien beings otherwise known as parents. How to pray on a streetcar. Being young, black, male and "at risk." Unrequited love in the motel strip. Pain—physical and psychological. The beautiful humanity of accidental encounters.

Welcome to *TOK: Writing the New Toronto, Book 3*.

The stories, poems and drama that make up the third book in this anthology series bring to bear two stark truths. First, our experiences in life relate very closely to the colour of our skin or the thickness of our accent.

Second, the fundamentals of human existence are exactly that—fundamental. The Chinese and black families that Clara Ho and Aisha Sasha John write about experience the familiar push-and-pull tension between parents and their children; the difficulties of partnership between any two people exist whether they're in a same-sex relationship or a mixed-race relationship in the stories by Shila Desai, Loreli C. Buenaventura and Elpida Morfetas; encountering strangers can make us feel something outside the ordinary, as we are shown by Alissa York and Michael Redhill.

The hopes, fears, frustration and moments of grace that people juggle every day are achingly familiar from story to story, yet are individually informed by the fact the parents are Chinese or black, that the lovers are Greek or South Asian, that the encounters bring connection or pain.

These stories, poems and drama also show that dealing with other human beings—whether in the personal or the public realm—requires accommodation. A crowded urban space, and one as diverse as Toronto, requires a daily give-and-take with people who may look and sound differently than we do, but who share many of the same hopes and frustrations. And what a gift: there may be comfort in similarity but there can be startling energy in difference—if we are open to it.

TOK Book 3 presents work commissioned from Michael Redhill, Alissa York, Molly Peacock and Judy Fong Bates through the Diaspora Dialogues publishing program. It also includes exciting new writers and poets discovered through an open call for submissions and nurtured in mentoring programs. The anthology expands this year to include a short play for the first time, and future editions of TOK will continue this hybridity in art forms.

Diaspora Dialogues creates inter-artistic and inter-cultural bridges. Programs encourage the creation and presentation of new fiction, poetry and drama that explore "place" in Toronto through lenses as diverse as the city itself. We believe writers of all cultural backgrounds should be given the opportunity to come together as artists first, and to connect with each other and with new audiences across cultural and disciplinary backgrounds.

The work offered here comes from a range of artists and is as varied in tone and presentation as are the writers themselves. Some of the pieces are overtly concerned with social justice issues or cultural or religious identity; others are subtly subversive. The writers are young and not so young, gay and straight, newcomer and established Torontonians. In short—they are the diverse folks who make up the citizenry of the city of Toronto.

Enjoy what they have to say.

Helen Walsh

Mo

Wasela Hiyate

Mo cannot take Fridays off. As a result he finds himself praying in the eastbound streetcar on his way to work. He assumes the appropriate position—as if holding the Qu'ran in hand—and enters a meditative state of worship, mumbling to himself at points where he usually sings when in the privacy of his own room. Mo makes time for prayer five times throughout the day, which isn't difficult since he is assistant manager at his uncle's restaurant and his uncle is a somewhat religious man himself. The plan, explained as such by Uncle Iqbal involves 1) gaining experience with Canadian clientele, which will enable him to speak English more fluently, 2) practising the most recent accounting software and techniques, and 3) giving Mo Canadian work experience. "Very, very necessary," insisted Uncle. "It was bad enough when I first came; you might as well have come straight from the tea plantation! But these days don't you dare grow a beard. You know what happened to Yusuf..." Uncle paused, looked thoughtful. "We'll just keep calling you Mo."

Once the few objectives Uncle outlined are achieved, Mo will be able to find a suitable position as an accountant with a good firm and make use of the diplomas he attained in Pakistan. "It will be difficult for you." The older man tried to comfort Mo with an arm on the shoulder. "It is not like home. Everything here is what they call *ass backwards*, you know. The gays have so much power. They are always on television with their supermodels. Reporters hang on their words longer than the bloody prime minister's!"

Mo finds the Canadian language difficult. Not as familiar and proper as the British English he learned at school. He always heard the word *proper* itself in the accent of his teachers in the past. There are many confusing terms and phrases, and he cannot guess how long his uncle's goal will take. Mo finds the language is even sillier—more silly?—when referring to food. There were a few products that his British teachers mentioned, with names that made him feel like retching when translated literally. Headcheese. Blood pudding. Or was it black sausage? The latter always made him think of a phallus filled with blood. But in Toronto, the supermarket where Uncle usually shopped was more *haram* than a brothel. Mo saw all types of references to the scavenger animal: pork hocks, pork bellies, pig knuckles. They minced it with fat and cartilage and sold it as sausage. Uncle insisted he could never bring himself to eat such monstrosity, while Aunty laughed in the kitchen behind him. According to Uncle, all the family restaurants also served the delectable—detestable?—hamburgers and cheeseburgers made with ground-up beef. Even the Hindus would have trouble eating out!

Mo does not understand food in this country. That people with money and some degree of education would enjoy eating their own or other people's pets, minced up in the same fashion as pig and sold on street corners as "hot dogs," makes him hang his head in great embarrassment for Canadians. It seems that people take their dogs very seriously so it does not make sense. And the sheer variety of dogs—wild and domestic—was shocking: poodles, dachshunds, Labradors, Alsations, Dalmations, St. Bernards, beagles, cocker spaniels...Once at the subway station, Mo had seen a black woman in boots and a red scarf walking a dog past a man seated on the floor. The man had moved, stirring about the crumpled newspaper and clothing that surrounded him, and started growling suddenly, scaring the woman. Her dog had barked back at the angry man. Then the man had started yelling about the wild dogs—something about trying to keep out the Chinks, wops, Yids, niggers and spics. They must really be savage beasts for him to have spit the names with such venom. Still, Mo knew about the raccoons, moose and the awesome white polar bears, black bears and grizzly bears, but who would have known that there were packs of wild dogs in Canada too? Perhaps so many of them died each winter that the government was compelled to sell their minced bodies as hot dogs.

It was not just the dogs of the culture that perplexed Mo. Some of the restaurants he'd dined in when meeting his English tutor made his heart heavy for the suffering Canadian people. The university chap always ordered a beer and small bony pieces of chicken wings that greased his lips so they shone throughout the tutorial. Shawn was very interested in teaching in Japan where rich and beautiful women supposedly awaited him. The restaurants he chose served dishes in which spices and herbs were replaced by the heaviness of sugar and salt. And the preferred sauce was a thick red liquid in a bottle that was both sweet and tangy, called ketchup. Canadians oozed—used?—the stuff over everything. Mo watched in fascination while Shawn drowned a plate of french fries in ketchup and vinegar. The tutor responded to Mo's incredulous stare, "What? You have curry sauce; we have this."

Even worse than eating in the restaurants was what came afterward—the toilet. Mo tried to hold it in during tutorials, but once, during the second meeting, he found himself so uncomfortable and bloated he couldn't concentrate on what Shawn's shiny lips were saying. Having to use the public stall was no problem, but using the paper to smother his waste like peanut butter had been so offensive that he'd cut his tutorial short—in the middle of learning the various rules and usages of the present progressive tense. He'd taken the subway directly to Uncle's house where he'd been given a room in the damp basement, and washed in the shower at a scalding temperature until he was satisfied. Mo lay on his bed, listening to the din of Uncle's sons upstairs cheering loudly in front of the television set, and Mo cried like a child. Nobody had told him it was going to be like *this*. Now he understood why others who'd gone off to the States called home in tears of frustration, telling family how terrible the living was. It was difficult to do anything in this part of the world *properly*, even keep your bottom clean! If only his mother would visit. She would coo kind and reassuring words, and her cooking was so much better than Aunty's. Mo prayed with each *namaz* for a visit from his mother or, second best, for a wife.

Mo understands that what this new society may lack in cuisine, it certainly makes up for in friendliness. In this country, everyone works together. His uncle's restaurant is a good example of this Canadian "cooperation" since the cook is a friend from Karachi, the porter is from Afghanistan and the dishwasher is, unbelievably, a Hindu from Kerala.

Mo looks up through the streetcar window instinctively, a block before his stop. He pulls the cord and fights his way to the rear door. In the restaurant, Mo finds everyone in front of the television in the kitchen, watching the afternoon report. The American president comes on and there are groans, pieces of misshapen naan and small chicken bones thrown at the screen.

"My dog's testicles contain more intelligence than that fool," Uncle says.

The waitresses roll their eyes when they catch a glimpse of the screen while placing their orders. They're all Canadian girls Uncle Iqbal hired based on their height and grace. He thought it made good business sense to hire white food servers in a country where most of the customers would be white. "One of them is even Jewish," Uncle had announced proudly. She had long ringlets that she shook free from her ponytail at the end of each shift. Mo noticed she also had the largest breasts of them all, a constant, though perhaps pleasant, distraction for his uncle.

"Ask the waitresses to wear these—new policy," Uncle said, a week after Mo was introduced as the new assistant manager. He handed Mo an assortment of colourful salwar kameez outfits with matching dupattas. The waitresses seemed delighted, paraded around in the flowing garments with the gold-embroidered dupattas draped around their necks. Sara, the waitress with freckles and short red hair, took to wearing her tunic with jeans on the street to and from the restaurant during weekend shifts with the scarf wrapped regally around her shoulders. She admitted that she sometimes wore it while out on Saturday evenings.

Once Mo asked Uncle what "butt" meant, after seeing a commercial on television in which youngsters repeated the phrase "Butt out!" while mashing their fags underfoot. Uncle had pointed to Sara's backside saying how *that* was a butt, fondling the fleshy flanks with his eyes, smacking lascivious lips. Sara often gave Mo peculiar looks, and once, blue eyes bright with interest, asked him about the mysteries of Allah. Such a direct question by a subordinate of high status—a white woman raised in the West where he understood everyone had many assets—made Mo panic, found him tongue-tied. He mumbled something unintelligible. The girl was visibly disappointed. It was then that Mo realized that he was not quite himself in English. He would have to practise making his tongue do the strange tricks to make the Canadian sounds, to be understood. More importantly, he would have to practise getting comfortable with Canadian women. But Mo does not understand them.

They look at him during the lunch buffet offered at the restaurant. His uncle has already told him they will find him erotic—exotic? "You are blessed by our side of the family's good looks: of course you'll get some attention. These women are attracted to tall men in properly cut suits," he said, picking lint from his nephew's lapel, "since they work on Bay Street."

"Aaah, Bay Street." Mo nodded to his uncle, feigning understanding. People trust a man who understands things, or at least looks as if he understands. His father told him this before Mo's departure from Pakistan. He also warned his son that American women were always falling in love. "They are crazy. Do not get involved. Sex-sex-sex and then *no children*—very strange. Your mother and I are looking for a suitable match for you right now. The proper family and age, sweet and ripe as a mango, fair as a dove. We will send her to you as soon as you have settled in and can support a family."

Uncle nudged him whenever Helen, the young woman from the insurance agency across the street, came into the restaurant for lunch or dinner. She was particularly friendly to Mo, complimented his cheerful accent, the length of his eyelashes, the whiteness of his teeth. At first he was shocked by her forward manner, even more so by the true yellowness of her hair. When he expressed his fear of the woman with doll's hair from the insurance agency, Uncle laughed with his whole belly calling him infidel—imbecile? Then the older man leaned over as if to impart great words of wisdom and said simply, "She is white all over, and in some places, *pink*."

Mo gasped, remembering pictures he'd seen once, belonging to chums from school. The idea of the different flesh and pink refinements made his phallus grow large, like a blood sausage. He was surprised and flattered when she asked him to accompany her to a restaurant Friday night, where they would eat some kind of sea creature that, to Mo, sounded like the name of a woman. Tamari? Calamity? Calamari? That was it.

"Do you like seafood?" she asked.

Mo nodded dubiously, leaned over to take her plate.

"Good." Helen covered his hand with hers. "Did you hear about the boy in B.C. who killed himself? It was on the news at noon. The kids at school called him a terrorist because his mother wore a hijab. It's so sad—he was only twelve," she squeezed Mo's hand and her lips pressed together in sympathy.

Mo tells this piece of news to Uncle and Aunty once the dinner rush slows down. Uncle heaves a great sigh. He closes the restaurant early that evening, lets Hari, the cook, the porter and the waitresses go, and the rest of them kneel on the Persian carpet facing Mecca, pray as the sun disappears from the sky. Uncle and Aunty shake their heads, leave the restaurant after Mo offers to check the stock for tomorrow and take care of the cash and float. He puts on one of the CDs Uncle bought during his last trip to little India—the latest film soundtrack. He whistles as he counts and coins fall into the deposit bag in time with the beat of the chorus.

After dropping the bag into the bank slot, Mo continues down the street. The streetcar, he decides, will take a long time, and he often feels stifled in the train carriages and the subway stations with their tiled walls—like gigantic bathrooms. Mo hears his dress shoes slap against the pavement. He comes to a nice neighbourhood, where many of the brightly painted houses display flowers and shrubs in the front yards. The smell of jasmine floods the street and Mo almost stops in the middle of the sidewalk, remembering the *chambeli* of his mother's garden. He is filled with a sudden wave of longing and thinks about the boy who was bullied at school. This is such a confusing place: bounteous, wonderful, cruel.

Mo turns the corner to find an older gent in an overcoat loping along the street. He turns suddenly and, in the light of the streetlamp, Mo sees the man smile at him. Mo is caught off guard, but manages to smile back. The tree branches sway in the night breeze and he looks around the neighbourhood, sees the warm glow in people's windows as they go about their business watching television, reading, playing with their children. Mo gulps the fresh night air in the deserted street. He feels a calmness he remembers from when he was a child. After waking early, before anyone else in the household, he would open the window and survey the sky; the sun peeking over the horizon and the peace of the morning would make his eyes water with a strange joy. There would be just a slip of fragrance from the jasmine before it closed itself for sleep during the day. Mo considers the unexpected beauty and brutality of the world, that these two forces exist together, side by side. He feels a dull ache in his chest, pushes his hands into his trouser pockets and walks all the way home.

On Friday evening, Helen meets Mo at his uncle's restaurant. Her hair is windblown back from her face in two feathery curls. "I'm sooo relaxed now. Just went out with some of the colleagues for a few drinks, and Chardonnay always puts me in a very good mood." Her eyes sparkle.

Mo is unsure how he feels about her having consumed alcohol, especially on a Friday. But he knows that a drink before the weekend is an important aspect of being Canadian and decides he will partake of this wine ritual at dinner.

As Helen drives into the parking lot beside the restaurant, a black sports car pulls up so close to them they can hear the music pounding from the vehicle. Suddenly the rear window opens and a large set of pasty buttocks bulges out.

"Butt out!" shouts Mo, pointing at the downy cheeks. "Now I get it. People are so in love with the bum in this country. No wonder homosexuals have such power!"

Helen can't look away from the horror of the full moon in the parking lot.

Minutes later, a waiter dressed in a white shirt and black trousers brings Helen and Mo a platter each of the calamari animal Helen has been talking about, with a serving of rice and grilled vegetables. Mo chews the rubbery creatures. He silently counts the number of them left on his plate, and smiles at the smiling woman sitting across from him. An idea seizes Mo that makes him want to spit it out, and he does so, discreetly, into his napkin.

"The creature makes an argument in my belly," he says, grimacing. "It is not agreeing with me." The fried calamari seemed to him like the elastic ring of an anus: perhaps of a cat or dog? How easily this restaurant fools the unthinking Canadian people. He wonders if it might be rude to tell Helen that right now she was probably eating the sphincters of various animals. Mo twirls the leaves of lettuce from his plate on his fork, letting the salad dressing drip, and decides not to mention it. He stares in fascination as she eats happily, taking long sips of wine from her goblet, giving him looks that make him uncomfortable in the pants. Mo finishes his serving of vegetables, his sweet salad and salty rice.

Outside the restaurant, Helen takes his hand. Unfamiliar with this kind of display of affection, Mo smiles, stiffly swings their hands back and forth as they walk along the street, heading to the parking lot. Once there, they are greeted by the ruckus of a group of boys leaning against the black sports car parked next to Helen's. The boys argue boisterously and smoke cigarettes. Two of them are engaged in a wrestling match on the pavement. The one in a baseball cap takes long drags of his cigarette.

"Hey, Paki."

"Hey, stinky Paki."

"Go back home, Paki."

Helen clutches Mo's hand tightly. Mo is used to this sort of thing, although he wondered at first how these Canadian people would know the word *pak* that meant clean and pure—holy—in his language. He understood then that it was really true, what the commercials on television said about multiculturalism. The addition of the diminutive form, *turning "John" to "Johnny"*—he heard one of his past teachers explain—made their attempt at friendliness that much more endearing. His translation abilities of common expressions need more practice, but he understands the essence of what the fellows mean:

Hello, perfect friend.

You carry such a pure fragrance.

Safe return to your holiest of homes.

Mo repeats the boys' greetings the way he always returned them—not wanting to be impolite—with a wide, friendly smile.

The young men look puzzled, glance at each other uncomfortably. The wrestlers stop for a moment. The smoker shrugs, takes a few short puffs of his cigarette and punches one of his friends in the arm.

Mo pulls Helen along to her side of the car and opens the door for her. She looks at him mournfully, wobbling on her high heels. "I am sooo sorry."

"It is perfectly fine, I will be better tomorrow," Mo says, patting his belly, assuming she's apologizing for his calamari stomach ache. He helps her into the driver's seat and walks around to the other side.

When Helen leans toward him in the car, the neck of her blouse falls open slightly, so that Mo can see how white white really is. Her cheeks are soft, her breath is warm on his face as she gives him a drunken hug. He touches the blond strands of hair near her ear, carefully. They are softer than he imagined and he feels as if he's touching some rarely seen creature, like those he reads about in the simpler passages of wildlife magazines. She is very pretty—more than that. When he looks in her eyes, he sees the gentleness of perhaps a...doe.

When she drops him off, he cannot bring himself to kiss her as she desires—on the lips. Considering what has been in her mouth in the course of the evening, Mo gives her an affable peck on the cheek instead.

The next day, Mo decides he will put up a sign in the window of the restaurant. He is just about to paste it on the glass when Uncle Iqbal stops him. Nodding his head, the older man says in their language, "Yes, yes, I know what you mean, but I believe this would be more appropriate," Uncle says as he carefully paints White Out over the last word of the sign—sphincter. He prints the correct word over it.

"How is it you and I know, but these people cannot figure it out?" asks Mo. He takes his time making sure the sign is straight, then goes out on to the street, to see how it looks beside the menu and the stickers displaying acceptable credit cards—a white placard with words written in thick, black marker: In this restaurant we do not serve assholes.

"You can't have a sign like that in the window!" says Aunty when she arrives, hours later. "It will ruin business."

"Keep it! Keep it!" the waitresses plead.

"Hey, Iqbal. Great sign!" says one of the customers as he leads a group of laughing co-workers to their usual table.

Uncle raises a brow at Aunty. "We shall see then," he says.

Just then Aunty's friend, Muneera, comes through the glass door. *"Arragh! Your sign is very gutsy, Iqbal. I wouldn't have expected it."*

"Well, I can't take all the credit. It was Mo's idea."

Muneera eyes Mo. "Well, not just a handsome face! Listen," she lowers her voice and the lines of her forehead deepen as she leans into the counter. "They are deporting Yusuf. Without any kind of explanation. He still has another year left on his student visa!"

Mo knows the story: Yusuf was arrested in the middle of the night. They never told him what the charges were. It was like some strange film about the Second World War. Mo met Yusuf at an Eid celebration held at the mosque last year sometime. The young man appeared average in every way but it seemed anyone from Pakistan was under suspicion. Could he have been involved in anything? Mo didn't know his family or anything about him, except that he'd been in the country for two years and was studying at one of the universities downtown. The police had never given any evidence against him or a reason for why it was necessary for him to be in jail.

"I told his mother before he left, Let him come—we will take care of him. But how? There are no laws for him!" Muneera cries.

Aunty puts an arm around the woman. "We will stand together on this and write letters and make phone calls. These people are not unreasonable."

The dining room is already filling up with the lunch crowd and waitresses float by like butterflies in their gauzy outfits. Muneera starts weeping into her shawl.

"Now, now," Aunty says to her, then she gestures to Mo and whispers, "Go fetch a box of sweets."

Mo picks out the best unbroken pieces of burfi and ladoos, places them in a small box lined with wax paper and seals it with a piece of tape.

"Thank you, sister," Muneera opens the box and bites into one of the sweets right away. "Oh, so good. No point in dieting anymore, not since the arrest, anyway." She moves to the exit. "*Salaam aleikum!*" She says as she pushes the glass door open.

"*Aleikum salaam,*" calls Aunty. Peace be unto you.

That night Mo once again offers to close the restaurant by himself. He likes having some time away from Uncle and Aunty and their cool, almost arrogant children at home. The boys speak a language he does not fully comprehend, and usually socialize in front of the television or video game screen. "Dude! Beat your score!" He often hears them yelling from the kitchen.

Mo decides to walk home again, so that he might witness the kind of domestic happiness, so carefree, that people seem to enjoy in this country— their lives filled with ease and opportunity. Or is it an illusion? As he strolls through the dark downtown neighbourhood, the night breeze rustles the leaves of the tall maples around him. He tries to sink into the calm he felt that night when he saw the man in the overcoat, remembered that quiet, mysterious joy from his childhood—but the effort is too taxing. He can't stop the thoughts racing in his mind like wild dogs. They have already taken something from you if you only feel fear, he thinks. It makes him angry. His pace quickens and he can hear the hard clack of his shoes hurrying in the empty streets. Then all at once he catches the smell of *chambeli* in the street. Jasmine. He stops, feels his shoulders drop. The night opens to him. Mo is hesitant to take a step and leave the scent behind, but he continues slowly, hands in his pockets. He whistles the soundtrack tune from the restaurant, then an idea strikes him. *Tomorrow, I will tell them to call me by my name.* Whistling even louder, Mohamed makes his way home.

Rock Dove

Alissa York

"Miss?" His hand closes on my forearm. "You got time to help an old man?"

It takes me a second to see it—his eyes are useless.

"Miss?"

How can he tell I'm not a missus, a ma'am? Can they smell that deep?

He gives my arm a squeeze. "Hey."

"Sure," I say, a little too loudly. "Sure thing."

The IGA is nothing special. The produce section is better than some—the local Greek widows see to that, shaking bunches of rapini, squeezing garlic bulbs in their fists. The place is Greek-run, but the staff is pretty much a mixed bag. The women behind the deli counter all sound like they come from Russia, or else one of those countries it swallowed and spat back out. They're mostly older, but there's one about my age, a skinny brunette whose name tag reads Tatiana. Her face makes me think of the Virgin. Not the dough-faced blonde, the black-haired Madonna with the mouth. When she holds up a slice of ham for my okay, I nod no matter what.

"This your usual spot?" the blind man asks.

"Uh-huh."

"I go to the Loblaws, know where everything is over there. I was out this way for the doctor, though. Figured I could use a change of scene."

He loosens his grip, sliding an inch or two closer to my wrist. The sound he lets out is minor, but I know he's felt the marks everybody else can see. I brace myself for a show of concern.

"We near the walnuts?" he says.

"Walnuts?"

"In the shell. You know, bulk. They round here somewhere?"

I've never bought walnuts in my life. I could take or leave nuts in general, especially when they're bitter and shaped like little brains.

"The boy said they were here," he adds.

And so they are, in a row of clear bins on the far side of the potatoes and onions. "I see them," I say. "This way."

We make an awkward pair—me over-careful, shuffling like a pensioner, him loose and easy, as though somebody's leading him to the dance floor. He keeps hold of me while I tear off a bag, lift the lid and fish out the silver scoop.

"How many do you want?"

"You do a couple of scoops, then let me hold them, let me see."

"Okay."

They make a surprising racket—a wooden sound, but lighter, dryer. When he holds out his hands I place the bag there gently, like I'm settling it on the scales.

"Huh," he says, looking through me, "another half-scoop."

I do as he says.

"No broken ones in there, I hope?"

"No, sir."

He holds the bag in one hand, reaches in and rubs a shell with his thumb. "That's fine." He ties off the bag and stuffs it in the straw basket on his arm. "Next stop, pickled onions."

At least one of the stockboys is slow. They don't wear name tags, but I've heard the manager call him Billy. He talks to himself—sometimes even giggles—while he straightens soup cans or drags old cracker boxes forward and shoves fresh ones in behind. He's only ever spoken to me once, and then he couldn't seem to stop. It was all about some neighbourhood dog, how he was always bringing it scraps, even after it bit him through the fence. I thought I'd never get away.

One aisle over, the stockboy's fifty if he's a day. You can tell he's got a hate on for the carts. He's always kneeling down with his dust rag or stacking up boxes so they can't get by. His shelves are something, though. Perfect rows of tea and cocoa, cornflakes, canned peaches, jam. Never a hole where the quick oats or the Coffee Mate ought to be.

Pet food, toilet paper and cleaning products belong to a tall, tongue-tied guy with bad skin. He's forever dogging women with his eyes. Not just the young ones, either—wide-load mothers bending for boxes of Tide, one time a tanned grandmother holding tissue boxes to the light. Who knows, he might even turn his head after a washed-out bone rack like me.

Pickled onions are something else I've never bought. I know where the pickles are, though—not far down the slow boy's aisle.

On our way there, the blind man lets his hand shift like a sleeve against my skin. It doesn't hurt or anything—most of the scratches don't even go deep enough to scar. I do my best to keep them clean, but you're bound to get an infection now and then. No such thing as a spotless claw.

"Okay," I tell him, "here we are."

"What brands they got?"

"McLaren's and Bicks."

"That all? Okay, McLaren's. Those Bicks might as well be marbles."

I add a jar to his basket.

"Good." His pale eyes search the space between us. "Sardines."

I should've guessed. I can't even stomach the smell.

It's hard to say which cashier is my favourite. Tia's the beauty—all those shiny braids hanging down around her shoulders—but there's more to her than looks. She smiles like she recognizes me, and not just from the last time I was in. Like she really knows me. Maybe one day I'll get up the guts to ask her where she's from.

Louanne's another story—nobody would ever call her good-looking. Her skin has a yellowish, slippery look. It must be her organs, kidneys or liver or something. When she meets your eyes it's like some poor animal staring up from where it's fallen down a well. And she's so careful. Always two rubber bands around the eggs, always a separate bag for any kind of soap.

In the end, though, I'd have to go with Giannoula. Not that she's an original choice. People line up three and four deep at her checkout when the others are free and clear.

Busy today, Giannoula?

Oh, you know, honey, off and on, off and on. They come and they go. You need a bag, baby-girl?

Thirty-odd years on the job and she's still got that crazy spring in her voice. You want to laugh when she talks to you, and not like a grownup at some stupid joke. Like a know-nothing little kid.

The sardines aren't far, same aisle, further down. We pass by Billy stacking garbanzos, talking in his private way. "Says he never, says he never..."

"Never what, I wonder," says the blind man.

He wants Brunswick brand in mustard, but they've only got them in tomato sauce, with hot peppers or in soya oil.

"Oh, go on and give me the peppers. I'll pay for it, but what the hell."

"How many?"

"Three'll do."

I reach down three flat cans. "Okay, now what?"

The blind man clears his throat. He relaxes his hand, lifts a long finger and waves it like the feeler on an ant. Slowly, thoughtfully, he traces the scabbed pattern on my arm. I hold my breath. He's silent for a time. Then, turning his eyes up at me, he says, "Birds?"

I don't know why I'm surprised—if he can smell married from unmarried, chances are he can pick up on bird shit. I clean the cages at least twice a week, but that doesn't stop them going all day long. Maybe he can smell the good side, too. The seed eaters give off something like fresh oatmeal cookies. If they eat bugs too it's sharper, not a stink or anything, just something you have to get used to. Meat eaters smell the strongest, but even that you can learn to love.

It's something I used to worry about, the house taking on their smell. There was even a dream I had, where Mama woke up from her grave and came flying at me down the narrow front hall, cursing and holding her nose. I used to pack my clean clothes in garbage bags, wash my hair before going out, even chew gum in case the air of the place had somehow fouled my breath. I don't bother so much anymore.

"You guessed it," I tell the blind man. "Birds." Next he'll ask me what kind—*budgies? parakeets?*—and I'll have to try and explain. Or else I'll have to lie.

"Let's see now," he says. "Eggs. Half a dozen, the brown kind if they got 'em."

I can't help but smile. Finally, something we both like.

I've never kept a healthy bird—the second they're better, I let them go. It's not as though I go looking for the hurt ones, either. It's always been them coming to me.

My first was a house sparrow. I was little, maybe six, walking back from mass with Mama, when it bounced off a neighbour's porch window and landed on the sidewalk at our feet. I crouched to pick it up, but Mama hauled me back up by the wrist.

It was as much as my life was worth to open the side gate and leave our yard, but I had a brave streak back then, and I was just tall enough to reach the latch. The sparrow was seven houses away—I'd counted on my fingers to be sure. It didn't move, but I could tell living from dead the second I laid a finger to its throat.

That bird turned me furtive. I stole a shoebox from Mama's closet, ripped up turf in the yard's back corner, even raided the next-door bird feeder like a greedy jay. I walked on cat's feet in my bedroom, and waited till I could hear Mama washing dishes or saying the rosary before I dragged the box out for a peek. Three whole days passed before the sparrow was strong enough to beat its wings against the cardboard lid. I might've been young, but I knew there was only one thing to do.

They've been finding me ever since—herring gulls dragging lures, pigeons with broken beaks, mangled or missing feet. Poisoned jays and grackles, dozens of stunned starlings, even the odd eastern bluebird. One time, a clutch of great horned owlets. One time, believe it or not, a red-tailed hawk.

Not all of them get to me in time. Crossing Gough Street last week, I came within an inch of stepping on a pigeon. It must've taken the wheel head on, because its insides were squished out around its feet. Rock dove, I remember thinking, the most variable plumage of any bird. This one was speckled grey and white around its flattened shoulders, its twisted neck. Its open wings were charcoal, except for the flight feathers, a pair of snow-white blades.

We get the eggs, then a bottle of Rogers golden syrup, then it's back to the produce section for a couple of pears.

"Sorry," he says. "I'm pushing you round like a lawn mower."

"It's okay, I'm not in a rush."

The truth is I can't even remember what I came in for. Not that it matters. If you walk the aisles there's always something—a box of J-Cloths, a new toothbrush, that popcorn you make in the microwave.

He wants the pears with a hint of red in them, so the colour must be something you can taste. I pick out one on the soft side, the other a little harder. "Perfect," he says, feeling them. I know for sure now he lives alone. "I do believe we're done."

"Oh," I say. "Okay."

Suddenly I don't feel so good. It's in my throat, that feeling you get when a cold might be starting there. Or when you've been keeping something to yourself for too long.

There are things I could say to the blind man. I could tell him about the sparrow I saved, or the pigeon I couldn't, or even about the crow I'm nursing now. I doubt her wing will ever come good—it hangs from her shoulder like a dirty old coat. I don't know if she hopped up onto my porch from the road or dropped out of the elm tree, but she was waiting for me like a package when I got home.

I could tell him everything. The way Mama always seemed to come at me in the hallway, alive or dead. The way the floorboards there still cry. I could go on and on like Billy the stockboy, until he has no choice but to nod and smile and begin backing away. Instead I lead him to Giannoula's checkout. Lineup or no, it's the best choice for a man with no eyes. I want her to call him honey. I want him to hear that voice.

Poems

Samantha Bernstein

To Toronto

I must love you quietly, embarrassed
by your unwieldy desolate sprawl, your cold heart
and shameless lack of fashion sense; deliberately love
what you have cobbled together so carelessly on gridded
streets predictable as a sitcom, the 1980s
a garish tattoo on your nether regions.
   (Had you been born beautiful, a sultry New Orleans,
gamine Paris or majestic Damascus; were you known
for romance or elegance, or like Montreal were praised
for joie de vivre; if you would be less careless with your history,
wear it to advantage like other cities; had you
a compelling air of heartbreak and decadence like Berlin,
                then you would be something
                to write about.) As it is
I, at least, am yours, have spent a lifetime learning to know you, skittish
mongrel, ambitious tart: I stow my heart in Kensington
Market, in your warm red bricks, beneath the Danforth Bridge,
hoping time will treat you kindly and my
devotion be not worthless.

As I Was Walking from the Beth Tzedec

Outside the synagogue, the Forest Hill
Yom Kippur traffic havoc on Bathurst,
Amid men with frayed prayer-books and kippas,
Slim pampered wives, their daughters in Prada
Whose preciousness frightens me, I realized
This walk to our car, after the shofar,
Is September ending, marks a season's
Change. I wanted for you, love, my tall goy,
To see where I grew up, so you could know
Wherefore I loathed it, and it me, and how
Apart from it I felt, and was. Instead
A sudden joy, as though we were children
Sharing important secrets, and simply
Your knowing made the knowledge beautiful.

Sonnets for the Flower-Men

1.

The first came to our table as we supped
on dumplings to celebrate one year wed.
Middle aged, from someplace warm, he shuffled
through with his bouquet, above which hungry,
gentle eyes proposed gifts, husband to wife:
a rose? We smiled, shook our heads no. He passed
a second time; my darling noted how
I trailed the man's stooped frame and shabby suit
(trying not to cry: that left arm held out,
flowers cradled in the right, like something
precious, as he bent toward unseeing
patrons). The price was absurd, but my man
paid; the vendor gave us a fond look, said
Thank you, you are the first; and gave us two.

2.

The other was young, a quiet smile fixed
above a slight body, which wore its long
hours and cheap black suit as though no other
option existed, and without umbrage.
Trumpet cries, smoke and talk drifted above
Kensington and this lone boy offering
lights twined to the stems of frozen roses.
He passed unseen or refused through streetlit
dancers and groups of young friends; yet he seemed
sure the night would have use for him: to hawk
flowers is a job, therefore a service.
He humbly offered romance, having not
walked long enough to know our desolate
raw crossroads of sentiment and commerce.

Industrial Evolution (A Reprise)

1.

The slow, sad days of your leaving: the knowledge
that soon it shall all be complete, and winter's pigeon-coloured sky, released
      from the concrete blocks of this old warehouse, will
no longer hover above the rustling grove of poplar trees that shimmer on the margin
of the gravel factory lot beside the rusted CP bridge
      to alight on this black ash and book strewn desk, at whose
          centre sits the monitor and its memory: command station, receptacle
of megabytes' worth of perspectives on life
lovingly collected and created by the dwellers of this home. The rooms will be emptied,
walls abolished. Every joint you joined,
      every board supported by your small, resilient frame,
      the honey-coloured floor you tore up decayed linoleum for, all will be razed,
become nameless relations
      to abandoned bed frames, filthy toys, the refuse of millions.
No eyes then
      will praise this greying light, this bleak, muddy
                  beautiful view: this scene
will be committed to the private dream of history: mine, yours,
some few others whose days were framed by this eaten, fissured wood,
      these rattling panes, a lifetime older than us.

2.

Who else, I wonder, wanders these rooms
in those strange quiet moments of unbidden memory? Maybe
      some rough, unlucky woman who crashed
beneath the red neon Toshiba sign light
      shining through the grimy window decades ago.
Or some old, old man whose hand gripped the wooden banister each morning
the years he fought the Second World War from between these walls,
      maybe wishing the grinding machinery of his days was something more
                  perilous, brave
or maybe content in this sunny room, marking time by the train whistle,
punching his hours in and out, industry clanging in the busy yard below;
      happy to spend lunch hours smoking at the stainless steel Canary bar,
                cold beer and a newspaper
whistling back through the wide streets and narrow bridges
      of the city's southeast end. And then
there is you and I

my first time in that room, the ludicrous youth of our joined bodies,
the only way we knew to say hello, that neon glow a seedy aphrodisiac
through the uncovered window.
We were seventeen:
what did it mean then, that urban gleam, my memory's body leaning into your taut back
that day beneath the Gardiner overpass, motorcycle fumes our alms to the sun as we
                              raced east toward your strange, your only home?

3.
I was captivated by your unnatural freedom,
by the high, bare space that contained your days,
each detail of your home's history and construction, the point in the wall that had briefly
                              been one with your thumb. Drums
and bike your only possessions, those and a brain that could microscope the cells
of bureaucracy into a ramshackle structure, ragged and permeable. Your life,
                              Ty, was a Byzantine city,
full of dark corners, sudden beauty, unbreachable histories;
you were only a savvy urchin
in the complicated streets, scamming passage through the lairs of Privilege.

Such a maze of a quest: forms, requests, debt, tests, dreams wheedled down
to official statements of purpose, only to begin to become someone
                              who may someday know
Medicine. North star, this distant quivering constant in your cluttered sky was navigation
through the noumenal paths of your desires, guided you again and again to the same
                              hidden warehouse of your own will
where I could find you soldered to the beige couch, laptop welded to your thighs,
punching out the clackety-clack of your accidental ascension at least one social class;
      your school peers a motley parade of comfortable kids with comfortable brains,
           none of whom ever gave a stoned anatomy lecture
           while making gourmet salad dressing or hauling drums up rickety stairs.
But you did, so many times
           they quiver before me, a kaleidoscope, a honeycomb
                              of mornings and nights nestled at home
in the belly of the city. My lover and yours
your room mates, after dinner was all joints, David Attenborough films, Tom Waits,
Futurama and debates: science, politics, art, philosophy
                              the various axes around which we spun
in a chaotic kind of unison; our lives dreamed up and seriously played
as any children's secret treehouse game.

Beyond our nest downtown's sleek towers were impervious grownups: distant,
unheeded, their stoic industrious bustling an admonition at which we giggled invisible
                                                                    and proud,
their vertical lives etched like roads into our minds'
maps of places we would never go.

4.
Now, having left Toronto, flown in fact so east it's west,
where you have your stethoscope and white coat at last,
         you come visit me on the Bayview Extension we used to delight in
         chicaning down, getting stoned, yelling over wind and CBC;
I find again our nocturnal glee speeding beneath the Danforth Bridge
lit by the night's last train or silent and steadily bearing its suicide blockade
         that looked to us below like rows of luminous crosses;
and passing the shuttered Brickworks, where men now dead
made the red bricks that in my lover's dreams mean home,
         I see the shades of you and me, Ty, at seventeen
         scrambling up the embankment there,
                  in morning's first hours
                  with no fear of slipping or being
                                    caught.

5.
Like so many urban children of the late industrial age, decay for us was an aesthetic
pleasure, refuge from the raw world of progress.
         To us, a crumbling overpass
or forsaken dockyard behind chainlink fence speaks disproven but beautiful
Ginsberg dreams, Benzedrine revelations in a nation full of promises
         and diners where truckers eat cherry pie and smoke cigarettes,
         talk to a buxom waitress named Dolores;
a world where romantic kids could for the first time love
rooftops at dawn and alleyways, embrace grit without wincing at the cliché.
         Though we knew it had all been done before,
this didn't destroy the sweetness of our nighttime communal ablutions
         in the vast bathroom with the rust-coloured floors, or the beauty
of climbing the wooden ladder at night to the platform that hid Michael's old, hard bed
beneath the sloping white roof. For there waited the tousled, long-limbed boy I love,
         and love binds us to this old, used world
                  and all its told stories
                  yet makes everything new.

On that ladder, water cupped in one hand,
I knew gratitude:
Toshiba sign a brief splash on my thighs in the blue city light
streaking beneath and between the stuck, dirty blinds,
I gave thanks
for the joy of my sturdy frame balancing upwards, this treacherous course
memorized over so many nights;
for these solid bones, muscles' complicity with my desires.
Young skin bared to the luminous blue, to these drafty concrete blocks,
their dust and epic spider's webs,
I gave thanks
for these brief supple years reaching for sleep framed by breached wooden casings
and reflected in wavering panes
full of the dark quiet Valley.
                    Ty,
disentangling your phone cord was more difficult than I expected:
trying to comprehend the empty nest
        of your electrical necessities, the black, dusty wires a stubborn testament
to how much of your life was spent in this room, to the early mornings pulsing
a broken dial tone as you ignored messages and began calls on speakerphone,
        your administrative complexities bleeding through the drywall at 8 AM
The cord was stuck between two others,
                        I had to unplug, replug, and the raw cut on my thumb
bestowed by J.R. as we packed your drums
        made every tiny push,
        every connection
        and disconnection
                    hurt.
                You were gone then,
                        the day had grown
                                older than us, morning
stomachache jitters and sheen of no sleep, suspended tears, the tense gestation of
February rain
        an ancient memory, severed
                    by the replay again and again of your face telling me not to cry
at the check-in desk, your eyes
        older than anything, the goodbye in them a trapped Atlantic,
                a whole history of frightened boys before vast voyages.
Raised-browed vulnerable huckster, you weren't fooling me,
the world then like a tramp's coat seemed too large around you.

6.

As the city did that night after our last gig, drum haul done one final time,
instruments a sleeping band of strange animals

in the desert of the deconstructed room.
Morning I had opened the whole space to the winter sun,
as perhaps nobody had ever done since the factories closed:
it didn't matter who saw us now, precautions needless for one final month,
fake business licence unstuck from the wall, no more careful shams
for the city's inspections when we would in two days transform home into recording studio
replete with defunct machines borrowed from Long & McQuaid.

For these last days, all blinds on the six-foot windows facing east and west were raised,
blinds that for years shielded our sweet illegal domesticity from the ad-agency hipsters
and movie production crews we'd pass each workday morning, suspiciously fresh
with our wet, unruly heads, knapsacks flung on one shoulder.

That night your home felt imperiled, exposed,
a nest in a denuded tree,
highrise lights a predatory glimmer in the near distance.
The city was marching toward us through the brittle night,
and the old concrete seemed much older, as though it might shatter
in the rawness of this winter air,
the brutal clarity of the coming year.

7.

The room not as it was those first months, spacious, settled in itself as an old man
who knows what he's seen, waiting for summer's tender dusk to drift through
his quiet shadows; now the high black ceiling seemed a dark space above
an empty stage, the final show packed away.
Though behind my eyes a recurring image, a body in free-fall toward inevitable earth,
arms and legs flailing a useless resistance,
we packed and laughed, took photographs with January a filtered silver
through the naked panes: bathed in this strange light,
each of us glows like a visiting angel on a daytime TV show, and seem as staged.
The men speeding toward unknown lands, like stereotypes
Michelle and I cleaned, put lives in order,
her long, competent fingers prepared gracefully for tomorrow; the city's eviction notice,
maps for the Don Valley Reconstruction buried beneath important forms, plates,
passports on the old teak table.

Eastern Avenue will become a berm, an artificial hill
to guard new downtown condos from the Don River's floods every 150 years.

Poised on the frontier of our adult lives,
     aided by an absurd confluence of long-expected events,
     I knew this goodbye was kind compared to farewells said throughout centuries,
     final glances of homes and homelands,
          everything known abandoned.
Such a gentle displacement, this, in the face of history, I wondered
       that it could be so hard: after all, this city had given us
       our beloved grey steel factory door, our rusty bridges,
           woven our impromptu midnight music with passing freight trains'
           minor-key songs of bygone urban industry;
had let us tumble through our early twenties outsmarting authorities,
speaking ourselves into being through smoky, sunlit afternoons
like Kerouac characters I loved and believed in at seventeen.
Fortune had granted us eight years to play out our formative visions,
      had brought to fruition this urban romance,
         our industrial evolution.

The Only Detail That Matters

Stacey May Fowles

ONE

In our fifth roadside motel room Alice is standing in front of the mirror examining her face carefully. She is wearing nothing more than a pair of white knee socks with a tiny lavender bow stitched just above the back of each slender cotton calf.

While she studies herself her tailless grey and white rescue cat named Olive circles the perimeter of her ankles methodically. Alice stops applying mascara for a moment and leans down to scratch the animal's eager brow with her free hand.

The cat is not travelling well. We both knew this would be the case but Alice insisted and I relented.

This particular motel manager said *no pets*, but Alice managed to charm him just like she charmed the rest of them.

The rest of them. All of them. Me.

I have been in love with Alice and her ever-changing pair of knee socks for six days and two hours now. I have known her for four months and two weeks. I will not tell her that I am in love with her for another six and a half months, and by then it will be far too late.

But here in this roadside motel, with this mangled, rescued cat, I know this love to be entirely true. CBC plays the animated version of *O Canada* that they have been playing for as long as I can remember, a watercolour homage to national unity to end the viewing day. I change the channel.

Despite the fact that the CBC has informed us the day is over, Alice deftly applies her eye makeup while blinking into a pink hand mirror hung crookedly on the motel wall. She has secured it there with a wide piece of silver duct tape she snagged from a maintenance cart in the narrow hallway outside our room.

"I could never get lost in this hallway," she said after she tore the tape from the roll with her teeth. "I always seem to be getting lost."

To me, the fifth-floor motel hallway felt like the kind one would be marched down before an interrogation. I pictured myself being forced down it with a gun at my back—likely a neurotic symptom of my guilt.

But Alice was just so damn charming, so damn happy to have made it from the noise of Toronto to this quiet roadside motel room without being caught that I smiled as the tape dangled from her teeth. The duct tape was a necessity because she refused to apply her makeup in the bathroom. She was convinced the lighting was designed to make her feel ugly. I certainly never would have thought so.

"No one's gonna fuckin' ruin this escape for me by making me feel like a dogface," she said as she pressed the tape securely onto the wall, smoothing it out with her fingertips.

Now that the problem of bad lighting has been solved, I watch as she combines a mass of powders and paints, scrawling on each lid like she was spray-painting a filthy phrase on a brick wall.

My stomach feels as if it houses a number of small sparrows splashing in a puddle, the way I assume love should feel. I'd never felt it until Alice; the love I had with Tom was a feeling of mild and fading comfort akin to a hotwater bottle.

If I'm honest, I've all but forgotten about Tom. In the glow of the bad bathroom light and the flicker of too-early Sunday morning nostalgic television reruns, I am already trying to figure out a way to confess my lovesickness.

Clad in a too-small bath towel, I am carrying the weight of the world.

I am listening to a Frankie Valli tune on the AM radio, smoking a Belmont Mild, eating a bag of Cheetos and drinking a Diet Coke from the vending machine in the fluorescent lit hallway.

After a good half an hour—the time it takes for *The Facts of Life* rerun to reveal its moral lesson on the Christian Television Network—Alice finishes her theatrical preparation and collapses suddenly on the bed. Her mangled cat quickly follows, finding a snug place beside her. Within moments Alice is smoking a cigarette while reclining a mere foot from me, wearing those knee socks. Thankfully she has now found the modesty to coordinate them with boys' Wal-Mart purchased Y-fronts and a worn AC/DC T-shirt. She takes a sip of my Diet Coke and steals a few of my Cheetos.

In an attempt not to stare, I read the want ads in the free paper of whatever irrelevant town we're in (and every town is irrelevant if it's not a large round dot on the map in the glove compartment) and I wonder about the personal lives of typists and machine operators and telemarketers. As I read through the classifieds, I imagine I'm looking to rent a one-bedroom plus den or searching for a Lincoln Continental. My fingertips become newsprint-grey like the room. All this imagining of a more normal life makes me so tired that I lie back on the scratchy sheets.

"It's almost five." Alice says, standing up. "Let's get eggs. Full three-egg breakfast at some greasy spoon."

"You hate eggs," I reply.

"I hate everything. But a girl can try," she says, approaching the window. I watch as she closes the stained roller blinds and then quickly opens them again, blowing smoke through the open window of our non-smoking room.

The comment doesn't faze me—I've always been clear on Alice's quiet distaste for everything living—and anyway, her sudden passion for breakfast is getting those fucking sparrows splashing again. In fact, I yearn to tell her about my love for a single thing in knee socks standing a few feet away, in the hope that she will *try*.

"Yah, alright," I say instead. "Let's go get breakfast, Alice."

TWO

For the good of the narrative, I'll let you know some things about Alice.

Alice never talks about her father.

Maybe he was in a war. Maybe he's a trucker. Maybe he's in the Don Jail.

(Which one of these details would be most accurate when trying to explain a girl like Alice?)

Maybe Alice's mother is a waitress in a diner. Is a secretary at a Bay Street accounting firm. Is a schoolteacher. A single mother.

(What kind of history would form a girl like Alice?)

Maybe Alice has a brother. A developmentally disabled brother. A *retard,* she'd say. Age thirty. Mental age seven.

Maybe she took care of him.

(Or even better:)

Maybe, at age eighteen, Alice ran away from thirty/seven.

She ran away from taking care of all of them.

Maybe she was the kind of clichéd city girl who had to grow up too fast.

And maybe I met her at bar on College Street that played classic rock and sold two dollar drinks on Tuesdays.

Maybe I met her at the post office.

She was working at the bar.

She was working at the post office.

She was drinking a gin and tonic.

She was putting envelopes in neat little piles, licking stamps, soliciting signatures for package pick-ups.

I was drinking a Coors Light in a can. Tom's favourite brand of beer.

I was mailing a letter to a wronged lover. A lover named Tom.

And then I met Alice.

And then I met Alice.

THREE

Why we left:

It was Alice's dad or Alice's boss or Alice's brother or Alice's boyfriend or someone else's boyfriend or maybe even Alice herself. She never really told me why we had to run from the city like we were in some bad made-for-TV movie about good girls gone wrong. She just told me we had to go, and I said yes without blinking, without thinking.

Alice always had bruises—so many of them over those months that I couldn't count—but they were always clear to me despite the fact that each one was carefully covered with pancake makeup. Thighs, chest, upper arms. I even spotted a cigarette burn on the inside of her right wrist once when she was standing in my kitchen stirring a cup of instant coffee.

I was never clear on what had been done to her and what she'd done to herself.

By the time we were on the road together there was a violet mark on her jaw in the shape of a tiny crescent moon, a mark that seemed deliberate, like a purple-blue tattoo that you might call pretty if you didn't know its source. Every time we drove into a truck stop to buy snacks or gas up she would pull the rearview mirror toward her and reapply her makeup, blotting out the enflamed imprint with a carefully saturated sponge.

I'd help her with the marks on her back before we'd go out dancing on Richmond together. When she was fresh from the shower, she'd let the towel fall to her waist as she sat in front of me on the bed. I'd smooth the thick paste onto her skin until she was perfect again, hook on her bra, help her slip a dress over her head when it was too painful for her to do so.

"I gotta get out of here. Get to the coast. I need the clean of the coast."

Alice's list of reasons to leave might have included:

1. A beautiful South American boy with the longest eye lashes Alice had ever seen, who wrote songs about her and sang them at local bars, who moved in with her without asking, who eventually came back to her apartment after she had kicked him out, came over in the middle of the night wielding a half-empty bottle of seven dollar red wine and threatened to "cut her open" with a kitchen knife in hand, screaming about how she had fucked someone else.
2. A tall blond actor—the someone else she'd fucked—who did the voiceover for commercials about joining the Canadian military that still play on television. A boy who, when the condom broke, said, "Whatever, you're on the pill, right?"
3. A saxophone player with a U.S. passport who wanted to live in Canada, who called her long distance from the port of Barcelona to tell her that he loved her, he always loved her from the moment he met her, which she later came to learn meant I really need a place to stay.
4. A perpetually drunk and unemployed boy who enjoyed doing mushrooms with her, who played Twister naked with her, who lent her his favourite sweatshirt that she never took off, who had a tattoo of an anchor on his left calf and kept three ferrets as pets.
5. (There was a woman as well, a beautiful Greek woman who ended up living with the saxophone player, a woman with long black hair and an insatiable sexual appetite who was better than all the men combined, a woman she consumed until the taste of every man who had ever wronged her was cleared completely from her system. The story of this single woman, conveyed to me in motel room #2 when Alice had had too much Jack to drink, was the one story that gave me hope.)

Alice had lots of reasons to leave, but why I left Toronto is a little simpler and a little more complicated.

"It's too dirty here. I need to go somewhere clean. Will you come with me?" Alice asked me.

Maybe I was always the good girl and maybe I'm really a bad girl made for TV. It was a Wednesday afternoon. With an engagement ring of questionable quality on my left hand, I left work and got in Alice's car. I didn't even think twice about it. She called me at 2:24 PM and told me were leaving, and at 3:07 we left. I didn't explain, I didn't call Tom and I didn't call my mother. I just got in that yellow station wagon headed west, took my shoes off and put my naked toes on the dashboard. As she drove, Alice rambled on about every man who'd left a few bruises on that beautiful back.

But then there was Tom.

Beautiful, simple, Tom.

Tom asked if I wanted to get married and I said yes because it seemed the right thing to say. When it's too hard to explain the nos of love, you can end up confined to the yesses.

Tom got down on one knee in front of me at the Lahore Tikka House on Gerrard before I'd finished my chicken tikka masala, and as I looked down at that sweet dopey face I knew there was no possible answer but yes. I remember the other patrons clapped and cheered as he slipped the tiny ring on my finger. I wanted only to finish my meal.

Alice never asked for a yes or a no from me unless it was whether I wanted a three-egg breakfast at a greasy spoon or a Diet Coke from the vending machine.

When I finally did tell Alice I had fallen in love with her, she never spoke to me again. She disappeared completely, and the pain of that was far more intense than the fear of the altar that drove me to her in the first place.

For a while though, Alice and I managed to play a neat and tidy game of house in our ever-changing grey and beige roadside motel rooms of varying degrees of outdated decor, sharing bags of potato chips and Diet Cokes. At night we would curl up against each other in the sweltering summer heat, our hands entwined and bodies spooned, until our skin got slick and sweet with sweat and we had to pull ourselves apart.

Before we left I emptied the joint account Tom and I shared—the one we were using to save up enough money to have what Tom had called a "real wedding." Alice and I routinely dumped our dollar coins and crumpled bills on the obscenely kitsch bedspreads of motel Canadiana and counted how much we had left—everything pooled so Alice, Olive the cat and I could survive as long as possible, pretending the toughest challenge we faced was the question of what we might have for breakfast.

FOUR

I kissed Alice for the first and last time on the very same day real life caught up with us and our yellow station wagon headed west from filthy Toronto.

We were standing together in front of the motel's only pop machine, my hands cupped and outstretched in front of me while she tried to find exact change for her third Diet Coke of the day. After she'd managed to collect one dollar and fifty cents from my open palms, she smiled her trademark pink, lip-glossed smile and said thank you sweetly. Without thinking, I leaned in and I kissed her.

As I did, the remaining change that was collected in my palms fell from my grasp. Our kiss was accompanied by the steady symphonic sound of lost nickels and dimes—silver beavers and Bluenose schooners—descending the concrete stairwell.

Then she pulled away. "Don't be like the rest of them."

The rest of them. The list of reasons why she left.

It was the sadness in her face that struck me first, a dismay that seemed to suggest I had broken the rules of our game and as a result it had to come to an end.

She turned from me and began feeding quarters into the slot.

"Alice, I'm—"

"Don't. Just don't."

Alice punched the Diet Coke button with the side of her fist, collected the can quickly and walked through the lobby and back toward our room.

I thought about following her, but instead I got down on my hands and knees in the stairwell and began collecting coins.

When I finished, my pockets were full and Alice was long gone. I walked into the motel lobby to find Tom putting an engagement party photograph of me into the nicotine-stained hands of the bearded motel desk clerk.

And it was okay. Because Alice had already left me anyway.

FIVE

Tom forgave me as I predicted. I found out later that he created some elaborate story to disguise what had happened, a lie that I had gone to tend to a family emergency on the prairies. I had no family on the prairies and pretty much everyone knew that.

We drove in silence back to the city, back to the filthiness Alice had tried to escape, back to its classic rock bars, where people drink two dollar drinks on Tuesdays and its post offices, where people send letters to wronged lovers. On our way we had sex and slept in some of the same roadside motels Alice and myself had stopped in, and much like when Alice and I were together in those motels, we never spoke about why I left in the first place.

The most Tom said on the subject was, "She's a fucked-up girl," and we left it at that.

As previously scheduled, I walked down an aisle toward Tom at our "real wedding" that fall, my cold feet warmed only by my mate's ability to forgive and forget my love for that fucked-up girl. We never spoke of Alice again, left her and her memory there in the same roadside motel I was "rescued" from—the last place I ever saw her. She didn't reappear in my kitchen stirring instant coffee, nor did she appear at the wedding, as I had hoped.

In the spring I received a postcard from Vancouver with nothing but a phone number written on the back.

I knew it was Alice, that her and her yellow station wagon had made it to the coast unscathed, *clean*.

"Alice?"

"Yes?"

"I was in love with you. That was the thing that made me different from the others," I said, staring at the place in the kitchen where she had stood so many months before.

The rest of them.

"No. That was the thing that made you the same. Until that moment, the thing that made you different was that you didn't expect anything back."

That's the only detail about Alice that matters.

Sides

Aisha Sasha John

She was very pretty, the girl. Pity how thin her lips were. That was Tara's first impression. The door to the basement opened and for a moment, the dull racket of the party yawned alive. The girl was the first to leave and she did so passing not three feet from Tara's chair without so much as nodding her head. Tara was sitting in the TV room with a book in her lap, waiting for her son's party guests to leave so that she could confirm they weren't inebriated. As for the state of this girl, Tara couldn't tell—she'd passed by too quickly. By the time Tara closed her book and put down her reading glasses, the chime at the front door had made its tinkle. The girl was gone.

Tara forced her bare feet into a pair of runners, flattening out the backs with her heels. The girl was already halfway up the block, hugging herself although the night was sticky and warm. In the yellow light of the streetlamp, Tara noticed some redness on the backs of her legs. A rash?

"Hellooo!" Tara shouted. The girl continued walking; she was moving quickly. "Hello, there! I'm sorry, but I don't know your name. Wait. Please!" The girl stopped without turning around. Tara stepped ahead and faced her. Her lips weren't thin. It was her mouth that was tight. "I'm Malik's mom, Mrs. Carmichael. Let me drive you home, dear. Okay? It's late."

The girl mouthed *okay.* No sound.

Tara had the girl stay put and she walked back to the house alone. She drove to where the girl was standing, even stepping out to open the passenger door. But Tara closed it after her too gently. The door didn't quite shut but she left it. As they drove it rattled lightly, punctuating the silence.

"Where do you live...um...?"

"Sabrina."

"Sabrina? Sabrina. Where do you live, Sabrina?"

"Dundas West and Keele. But it's okay, you can just drop me off at the subway."

"Oh no. No, no. I'll take you right to your door."

The door kept rattling and to block the sound of it Tara turned on the radio. But the rattle was relentless and the music, if anything, highlighted it.

The normal thing for Tara to do would've been to ask Sabrina about the party. But Tara couldn't. The girl's distress was too obvious. Any casual inquiry about the night would have been false, insensitive, even. Prying. The girl's head, the point of her knees, her crossed arms—were all faced outward to the rattling door. It was the door too that received Sabrina's last words: *Thanks, Mrs. Carmichael. Bye.*

The next morning—Saturday—Tara's husband called home. Vincent had been in Vancouver on business since Thursday and wouldn't get back to Toronto until the following Wednesday evening. Malik answered the phone: *Yeah Dad, it was great. I had a lot of fun. No, no, no—nobody broke anything. Some pop spilled but I cleaned it up right away; you can't even tell. Yes, I'm sure, ask Mom if you don't believe me. Well, eleven including me. No, you said ten guests. No. I could've sworn you said ten guests. When they left? Oh, I'm not exactly sure, one-ish I guess. One-thirty maybe. Oh, Mom is saying one-thirty. Umm, she helped a bit but I did most of the cleaning, right Mom? 'Kay, love you too. Okay, here she is.*

"Hi, dear," Tara said. Malik was making a shake or something, slamming cupboards. The fridge door was ajar. "Malik! The fridge." She poked his side. To Vincent, "Sorry, hon. You were saying?" Tara hoped Malik would hurry it up. Leave. She wanted to mention the thing about the Sabrina girl to her husband. But as Vincent talked about his conference, Tara thought better of it. She'd be better off asking Malik first. Good chance the girl's behaviour had some really straightforward explanation. Tara remembered what being a teenager was like—it didn't take a whole lot to crush them. Someone could've told her she was fat, made fun of her outfit—it could've been anything, really. Right?

• • •

There'd been no discussion over what part of the house Malik would host his birthday party in. The basement was big and not easily damaged. The carpet was deep red plush; the walls, dark wood panelling. There was a small, shiny bar stocked with red wine and a few fancy bottles of rum. A badly lit hallway connected the main area to a tiny office and the door to the backyard. There was a fireplace down there too, and a worn leather couch littered with videogame cases, potato chip crumbs in its creases.

The party was small: Malik's dad had imposed a ten-person maximum. Any more and his mom would actually have to be present. Ten or under and she could remain upstairs and passively keep guard. So ten it was: five guys and five girls plus the birthday boy himself. The guys were old friends with the exception of Trevor's older cousin, in town from the States for a funeral. The selection of the girls, at his friends' insistence, had been more strategic: Cassandra and Sabrina—the two hot girls—and their joint entourage.

Malik sat on the arm of the couch, half annoyed, half intrigued by what Trevor and Kevin—his cousin—were talking about. From across the room they ogled Cassandra, who sat behind Malik in English. "Cassandra?" Malik said, "Whatever, man. She's too cocky."

The cousins screwed up their faces.

"Who cares if she's cocky, man? Fuck, her booty is *large!*" said Trevor, hi-fiving his cousin.

"Naw, man. I hate attitude. And her eyes are mad close together. Sabrina's way better looking." Malik found Sabrina interesting. She was the quasi-leader of the group. Kinda loud, a little bit bossy. But if anything, that was Malik's type.

"Yo, Sabrina's too much man. She doesn't know when to shut her mouth."

"Yo, which one is Sabrina?" said Kevin. Trevor pointed.

"That one? Guy, she likes me."

Malik's eyes rolled unwittingly. "Likes you? You don't even know her."

"Guy, she's been eyeing me all night. Trust me. This chick wants my dick!" Malik shook his head but he couldn't help but smile. Kevin was tipsy and obviously an idiot but he was forward and it was kind of refreshing. Except he'd been rowdy all night: throwing the Xbox controller at the wall when he lost a game, putting the music up really high right after Malik's mom yelled down to lower it.

In the corner beside the bar the girls were having some kind of dance contest. Cassandra looked bored and had her arms tightly crossed—as usual. Sabrina and the three other girls danced in a square. "Go CeCe, go CeCe, go!" they were shouting. Sabrina grabbed CeCe by the arm and forced her into the centre. CeCe dropped low and started popping. They cheered. And then CeCe's balance gave way and she fell, butt first. Malik caught the sound of Sabrina's laugh and looked in her direction. She met his eye and crossed the room.

"Birthday boy. What are you looking at?"

"Nothing. You laughing."

"Shit, Malik, am I *that* hot?"

Malik told her to shut up but not without blushing.

"You shut up," Sabrina replied, "Don't think 'cause it's your birthday I won't whup your ass." He made a face at her. She made one back.

Sabrina turned her attention to the cousins, whispering to themselves.

"What are you two smiling about?" She studied Kevin's face. "Hi, I'm Sabrina."

Kevin told her his name, grinning.

"So? Answer my question. What are you guys talking about?"

"They're talking about sex, Sabrina. I don't think you want in," Malik said, hoping to interest her by excluding her.

"Oh yeah. Well, what do you know about what I want, Birthday Boy?" And she plopped down on the couch, sandwiching Trevor between herself and his cousin. Malik, perched on the couch arm to Kevin's left, felt cut off. Then Kevin said something and Sabrina laughed. Malik missed it so he asked Kevin twice to repeat. He didn't.

Malik stood up and said, "Guys, I'm getting chips. Anybody want some?" Only Trevor shook his head.

At the snack table, Jay and CeCe were adding something from a flask to a plastic cup filled with ice.

"I hope that's vodka," Malik said. "'Cause if my mom smells it on you, I'm dead."

"Chill, Malik," said CeCe and she brought the flask to his lips. It was sweet. Coconut rum. He took the flask from her hand and had another sip. Jay put his arm around Malik and eyes on CeCe, he whispered, "Pretend I'm talking shit."

"Fuck you, Jay." She was laughing. "Malik, tell me what he said!"

"He didn't say anything. I swear."

"Yeah, right. Tell me!"

Someone's cell phone was ringing loudly on the table. Malik picked it up. The name on the caller ID was "Home." He flipped the phone open to figure out its owner.

"Oh, Sabrina's," said Malik. "I'll get her." He put the phone in his pocket and left CeCe with her finger wagging in Jay's face. But Sabrina wasn't on the couch anymore. No one was. The bathroom door was closed and Malik waited outside but it was Cassandra who came out and she was alone.

Malik made out Trevor's figure leaning against the office door down the hall. He walked over, asked about Sabrina. Trevor pointed to the office door without saying anything, eyes wide.

"What's she doing in *there?*" said Malik but before he even finished the question, he knew. Trevor shushed him and gestured for Malik to listen. He cupped his ear to the door and what he heard inside sounded like Kevin's voice. There was nothing of Sabrina. Malik reached his hand for the doorknob but Trevor slapped it away. "Are you crazy, guy? Why mash up the man's flow? You jealous or what?"

"Fuck you."

"Relax, Superman. Sabrina's a big girl. She knows what she's doing."

Malik wasn't sure what to do; he didn't trust Kevin. But then again, hadn't she snubbed him for Kevin earlier? So Malik left, Sabrina's cell phone still in his pocket. He put a different CD on the player and did another shot with Jay and CeCe. Anthony and Mohammed were playing dominoes on one corner of the bar. They were slamming the dominoes hard and it was loud; Malik was getting nervous. Trevor, meanwhile, stayed put at the office door, arms crossed. Like a guard, Malik thought. A lookout. A premonition he'd suppressed earlier came up in a flood.

Malik walked over and shot Trevor a mischievous smile. He put his head to the door for a second—as if listening—and then quickly turned the knob and just pushed the door open. The lights were off inside but he heard movement —shuffling around on the floor—and soon Kevin was in Malik's face.

"Hey man! You can't barge in on people like that!"

"It's my house, man! I can go wherever I want!"

Just then the door swung shut from behind and both Malik and Kevin were pushed out of the room.

Kevin said to Malik, whispering now but loudly, "What are you doing, man? How you gonna interrupt like that? Yo, you're tacky." Kevin nudged his cousin. "I can't believe your friend, Trevor." To Malik: "Man, I know it's your birthday and ting but damn!"

"Look, this is my house—"

"Yo, both of you, relax." Trevor said it with an air of finality. The two shut up—Malik, secretly relieved.

The rest of the party seemed oblivious to the commotion: the girls were singing now, their voices high and loud. The dominoes made their noise.

Outside the office door, Trevor suggested videogames. Malik muttered his agreement. Kevin said, "Fuck, yeah! Imma cream y'all!" Still, the shit talking that had accompanied their gaming battles earlier that night was absent. And though the couch had room, Malik stood upright to play; Trevor and Kevin were seated.

Midway through the second match Malik faked an early loss and while the others battled it out, he excused himself to pee and ended up at the office.

"Sabrina, you there?" He whispered at the door while tapping it lightly. No answer. He called her name again and pushed the door in slightly. The lights were still off.

"Sabrina?" he said again. It was dark. He couldn't make out anything. Malik hesitated at the idea of turning on the light but did it anyway. The room was empty.

He scanned the bar area for Sabrina. Nope. Trevor and Kevin were still at it, lost in a virtual war zone. Malik headed toward the bathroom again and found the door locked. He knocked after waiting a few minutes. Whoever was inside made no answer. He leaned against the door and when it finally opened: black and pink cornrows. Sabrina. He caught her eye for a moment and then she averted her gaze. Her face looked shrunken.

"Sabrina," Malik said, but she was already past him. He grabbed her arm. Sabrina jumped.

"Yeah?" She looked at him and it was Malik now who moved his eyes.

"I have your phone," Malik wrenched the phone from his pocket, holding it out in his palm so that *she* could take it from *him*. She did and put it into the pocket of her skirt. Sabrina walked toward the stairs, she walked up the stairs and then pushed the basement door open and was gone. The stairwell was bright; Malik noticed that the backs of her thighs were red. It looked like some kind of abrasion. Like carpet burn.

• • •

It was a little after seven on Saturday evening by the time Malik returned from his birthday shopping trip. He came home to find his mother clearing room in the fridge for a lasagne. Malik himself wasn't hungry; he'd already eaten at the mall. It had been a boom year as far as birthday gift money had been concerned. He'd bought: two golf shirts, jeans, basketball shoes, a videogame and two DVDs. Malik modelled one of the shirts for his mom and as he strutted around the kitchen, she held a wooden spoon to her mouth and played announcer. He offered to try on the other shirt for her even though the only difference between it and the first was colour. Malik's mom cut slices of birthday cake for them both, eating hers and complimenting him on the navy shirt, truly more sophisticated looking than the white.

"Malik, sit. Eat. We have to finish this cake before it gets stale."

"Ooh. You don't have to tell me twice. I thought I had to save some for Dad."

"He had his share at your dinner party. The last thing your father needs is cake, anyway. Besides, by the time he gets back from Vancouver it'll be dry."

"True. True."

"So, you like any of those girls at the party?"

"Mom! Come on!" said Malik, his thick brows rising.

"What? I'm just curious." Tara said, not quite smiling. "I saw some pretty girls making their way down those steps."

"Yeah, some of them ain't bad."

"Aren't bad, Malik."

"Sorry, Mom. Aren't bad."

"So is that a yes, then."

"Um...Let's call it a maybe."

"Okay, mister. Fair enough." Tara paused. Then, "What about Sabrina?"

"What *about* Sabrina?" Malik cut a chunk of cake away with the side of his fork and put it in his mouth, filling it.

"She's pretty."

"She's—" he swallowed, "alright."

"Oh come on, Malik. The girl's cute." His mom wiped the last bit of icing from her plate with the upper side of her pinkie finger. "Aren't you wondering how I know her name?"

"Not re—How do you know her name?" How *did* she know her name?

"I gave her a ride home."

"Oh yeah," he said the words casually but a sudden stillness betrayed his surprise. His mom pushed her plate aside and crossed her arms against her chest.

"Malik, did Sabrina enjoy herself at the party?"

"I don't know. Probably." Shit, Malik thought. Shit shit shit.

"Well, the reason I'm asking is Sabrina seemed a little, how do I put it—distressed, say—when she came upstairs."

"Oh yeah?"

"Yes. You can't think of why that might be, can you?" Tara leaned back on her chair, arms still crossed, looking at Malik over the tops of her glasses.

"Uh-uh," Malik said and shook his head.

"No, huh. You sure?"

"Yes, Mom. I'm sure."

"Okay then. 'Cause if anything happened last night that I should know about for sure you'd tell me, right?"

"Of course, Mom."

Malik's mom sat up from the table and gathered their plates, locking eyes with him as she left. He knew enough to hold her gaze but he looked nervous and he knew it. She put the plates in the sink and turned on the tap to wash them, her back now facing Malik. He asked to be excused but she didn't hear him over the running water.

"What was that?" Tara said. She didn't turn her head. Normally she would have turned her head.

"May I be excused?"

"Oh," she said, switching the faucet back on. "Yes, Malik Carmichael. You're excused."

It was Wednesday after 11 PM. Tara sat on the edge of their bed, Vincent's open suitcase at her hip. "You want to talk to the *principal*, Tara? Is that really necessary?"

"What do you mean, is it necessary? Have you not been listening to me?" Tara reached for his hand. He squeezed hers and then let it go in order to hang a shirt.

"Malik said she was fine, right?"

"No. Malik said he didn't know. That she *probably* had enjoyed herself. And even still, I mean—who knows? What does Malik know?"

"Tee, you weren't there. Malik was."

"He wasn't necessarily with every party guest at every second, Vincent. The basement's big."

"It's not that big. And there weren't that many of them. If something happened, I'm pretty sure Malik would've noticed."

Tara sat up from the bed to meet Vincent at the closet. "What if it happened in the bathroom, Vincent? The office? Behind the bar, even..."

"Oh come on Tara, this is pure speculation. So the girl looked a little tense and she ignored you. So what? Who knows what goes on with teenage girls? No offence, but it could've been anything."

"Vincent. I saw her. I saw her, okay? She did not look fine. In fact—"

"In fact, what? Relax, baby. Relax." Vincent kissed his wife on her forehead. "You're a little paranoid, Tee. You know that. I'm sure everything's fine."

Tara didn't say anything for a minute. She pushed a group of jackets against the wall to make more room on the rack. Half of what Vincent had just hung up was backwards. She righted them.

"Vincent, what if Malik is lying?"

Vincent shook his head. "Okay, now you're taking this too far. You give a ride to some drunk girl—or high, Lord knows what—and all of a sudden she's a victim and Malik's a liar? Relax, Tara. Okay? Just relax. I'm not talking to any principal. And anyway, if—and I'm only saying if—something *did* happen, don't you think this girl would tell whoever needs to be told herself?"

"No, of course she wouldn't. Think about it. And stop telling me to relax. You're the one who needs to check himself. Your wife," Tara was enunciating each word, "suspects a teenage girl got sexually assaulted in your own damn house and you don't want to do anything about it? I can't believe you sometimes, Vincent." Tara walked heavily toward the bed, pulled back the duvet dramatically and jumped underneath.

"Tee." Vincent looked at her with his hands open, head cocked to one side.

"Don't you 'Tee' me." She left the bed and went to the bathroom. Vincent knew better than to follow her. She came back smoothing cream around her eyes, her fingertips making small circles at the top of each cheekbone.

"Yes, I think Malik might be lying, okay? It's not like it hasn't happened before." Tara took a deep breath. "I need to get to bottom of this, Vincent. With or without your support—I have to."

"Tara, no. We're in this together," Vincent put his hands on her shoulders. "Come on."

"No. No way," Tara said, mostly to herself. "That girl is somebody's child, too."

"Look, I'll talk to Malik tomorrow and see if I can get anything out of him. Hold off on the whole principal thing for right now. Let me at least try. Tee?"

"I'm not making any promises. You just talk to your son." Tara lifted his hands from her shoulders and placed them at his side, deliberately. She got back into their bed and pulled out her book without saying another word. Ten minutes later she called his name. He was on his side of the bed putting on pajamas. He didn't answer. She called his name again.

"What?" said Vincent and his tone stung her.

"Can you turn out the light please?" This wasn't want she meant to say. She didn't have anything to say. She just wanted to hear his voice.

"I will. Holy shit. Can I get my pants on first?"

Tara returned to her book.

◆ ◆ ◆

The glory of Vincent's face was in his profile. Lips, nose and forehead all met at a straight line. The sense of geometry was exquisite. In good times Tara could feast off his face from any angle, but during their rough spots she liked to lie on her side and watch his profile as he slept. It soothed her. This was the way she fell asleep that night, their feet touching occasionally—nothing else. Vincent: stone, staring straight upward, his body rigid until softened by the wash of sleep. He came to her in the night, though. And then she felt him against all but the arch of her back. She awoke to him pushing against her, softly—embarrassed by his need. And they made a slow kind of love, eyes closed, Vincent sucking on the back of her neck.

◆ ◆ ◆

Malik's dad jogged on the treadmill in front of the evening news, his belly bumping into the front panel every few steps, face perfectly matte. Malik waited until a commercial to say *Hi Dad*. Still, the surprise made Vincent trip; he had to grab hold of the bar to steady himself.

"Whoa. Easy, Dad. Don't hurt yourself, now."

"Ha ha. Very funny. Sixteen is not too old for licks, you know."

"You'll have to catch me first, Dad."

Vincent made a fist at Malik, who'd already turned his head, missing it.

"Malik, I need to talk to you." Vincent turned off the machine and joined Malik in the kitchen. Malik was shaking a cereal box at his ear.

"Yes, Dad?"

"What's this about some Sabrina girl at your party?"

"Pardon?"

"You heard me. Your mother seems to think something might have happened to her. Like someone messed with her or something."

"She does?"

"Yeah, she does. You know anything?"

Malik didn't answer.

"Speak boy! Do you know anything or don't you? And if you do you'd better cough it up quick."

"I, um, I—"

"You've got five seconds, boy. Five. Four."

"Okay, Daddy. Okay, okay." Malik rubbed his temple. "She was in the office with some guy—Trevor's cousin. He's not from here, you don't know him. I pushed the door in and Kevin—the cousin—came out but she didn't and when I gave her her cell phone later she acted kinda weird. That's all I know."

"What were they doing in there?"

"Dad, I don't know. I didn't see anything. The lights were off."

"So wait, how did you know they were there in the first place? Don't tell me you guys were playing some kind of nasty game. Malik!"

"No, Dad. No. Her cell phone rang and I wanted to give it to her and I asked Trevor where she was and he motioned that she was in the room."

"How did Trevor know, then?"

"I don't know, the three of them were talking earlier. Trevor was, like, standing outside the door the whole time."

"Oh Lord," Vincent put his hand on his Malik's shoulder. "Tell me about this boy, the cousin."

"I don't really know him. He came from New Jersey for Trevor's granny's funeral. He's older though, maybe eighteen. He seems a little, I don't know—wild."

"What about the girl, she fast?"

"No, no, no. She's a nice girl. Smart."

Malik dropped his head.

"What son? What?"

Malik spat it out, sobbing now, guilt at full bloom. Sabrina had stopped talking to him. They were regular partners in Drama and for two classes now she'd ignored him, joining some other group. Malik himself wasn't really talking to Trevor. But that wasn't the worse of it.

"She had carpet burns on her legs, Daddy. I saw it in the light. I tried to get in there but Trevor stopped me and I just left. I don't know why, I just...I don't know. I don't know what happened in there, Daddy. I don't know. What if...you know...and I could have stopped it. What if, Daddy? What if?"

The following evening, Malik and Tara sat opposite each other at the dinner table, Vincent's seat vacant between them. Vincent stabbed tongs into a salad bowl before setting it on the table, the strings from Tara's apron—"Chef Mom"—dangling behind him. He pulled roast chicken and macaroni pie from the oven and placed them beside the salad before sitting down, apron still on. Malik said grace at Tara's request and they began eating.

"How's school, Malik?" said Tara.

"Fine." Malik's voice was muted, a whisper.

"Just fine?" said Tara purposefully loudly, wiping the corner of her mouth with a napkin.

"Yeah. I mean, yes, mom."

"Hmm," she said loudly again and continued eating.

"It's okay, boy, just eat your food," Vincent said to his son.

"What's that supposed to mean, Vincent? What, I can't talk to my son now?" Malik fixed his eyes on a slice of tomato.

"Tara, let the boy be, okay? You know he doesn't want to talk." Vincent took a bite of his food. "He's shook up."

"He should be *shook up*," Tara said to her husband, eyes on Malik. "That poor girl."

"That poor girl," she said again.

"Tara, enough. Okay?"

"Vincent Carmichael I am *not* your child!" Tara flashed her husband a look.

The cutlery scraping against the plates, the sound of Malik gulping his juice, Tara clearing her throat—these were the only sounds for the remainder of the meal. Malik—no surprise—was the first to finish and he excused himself meekly.

"Tara. If I didn't know any better, I'd swear you thought Malik was the one who messed with that girl. You're treating him like he's guilty."

"He is guilty. He's guilty of not doing anything."

"Tara, what did you expect him to do? Beat up the guy? He didn't know what happened. We still don't know."

"Well, if I suspected some foul play on one of my friends by some stranger, I wouldn't be playing video games with him two minutes later."

"Maybe that girl should think twice before going into dark rooms with strange boys."

"Oh please. Vincent, kids make out at parties, it's what they do. That does not give any guy right to violate a woman's boundaries. Do not go there. Please."

"Okay, fine. Sorry. But to put it on Malik is not fair, either."

"I'm not putting anything on Malik. It's clear who the perp is in this situation. But Malik should have at least opened his mouth and told. I hold him responsible for the fact that he didn't."

"Sure, of course. But you have to understand it from his perspective, Tara. He wasn't sure what happened."

"He knew enough to cry about it. He knew enough to lie to me bold faced. You baby him too much, Vincent. Don't you want him to grow up a man?"

"You just don't get it sometimes, Tara."

"Get what? Consistency? Integrity? What don't I get?"

"Mistakes. I know you're perfect, Tee, but the rest of us can only try and it doesn't help if you shit all over us every time we make one."

"Good one, Vincent. Good one."

"Malik knows he's done wrong, Tara. Okay? He knows."

"He damn well better know."

Vincent shook his head.

"Vincent, I don't care if you think I'm a bitch. I don't care if Malik thinks I'm bitch. It's my job to make sure that boy knows right from wrong."

"That's what I mean. You only see the one side. Malik needs more out of you than moral definition, alright? He needs your support. Your compassion, dammit. The girl was his friend, you know. Trust me, he feels way worse about this than you do, Tara. Way worse."

Tara got up from the table and carried her plate to the sink, knife and fork sliding across it. Vincent sat there, watching her. She rinsed the dishes and left them in the sink. Behind her Vincent hadn't stirred. Tara: "Are you gonna help me or what?"

"I cooked so you're cleaning, right?"

"Oh right. As if I don't wash up half the time I cook anyway."

"Tara if you have something else to say, say it. But I could do without the attitude."

Tara turned around now. Vincent was still seated, jaw clenched.

"What more do you want me to say? I'm disgusted that my husband's fine with our son behaving like a punk? There, I said it. You happy? I just don't get how you are so okay with this. So bloody *defensive* of Malik. This is how it starts, you know."

Vincent jumped up, his belly hitting the table edge. A glass fell over, spilling water onto the floor.

"How what starts? Malik's life of crime? I swear, Tara, sometimes I wonder about you. You think so *small*. Do I have to spell everything out? Don't you get what's at stake here? You getting the principal involved means the police could be next and who knows? All I'm saying is Malik did not *do* anything and I don't see what point there is in dirtying his name up with some situation—"

"Some situation! Some *situation*! Is that how you see this? The girl might have gotten *raped* for all we know, and you're worried about Malik getting— God, I don't even know what you're worried about—"

"You're damn right I'm worried about Malik! He's my son, dammit! If you weren't so goddamn busy playing *hero* maybe you'd be worrying about him too!"

"Jesus Christ, Vincent. Did you hear me? Rape, I said. R-A-P-E!" Tara banged her fist on the counter with each letter. "Are you fucking listening to me?"

Vincent just stared at her.

"Like, Vincent, come on!" She was yelling now. "Come *on*, baby!" And then she was crying and he felt the weight of her feeling. He felt the plea. Vincent held Tara, she was shaking in his arms, crying harder still. Then she pulled back and said:

"Baby, don't you get that I *am* worried about Malik. I'm worried about what kind of example we're—you're—setting. Shit, Vincent, I can't believe you *think* this way. I can't—"

"Tara. Baby." Vincent put his arms around her again. "Shhhh. It's okay, babe."

"No, don't shush me. Don't shush me, Vincent. I'm serious." She moved her head from his chest to meet his eyes. "Baby, do you *really* think it's more important that we avoid some kind of, I don't know—messiness— than it is that that girl gets whatever justice she deserves? Because I can't handle that. I can*not*."

"Look. I just don't like the idea of it, okay? I don't like the idea of it period and I especially don't like the idea of it having happened here and at Malik's party."

"What, and you think I *do*? You think I do, Vincent? But we can't ignore the fact of it just 'cause—"

"Yeah yeah, I know. Okay. I know. I'm sorry." Vincent moved her from his body to take hold of her hands. "Tara, I'm sorry. I am. Okay?" He said it again, and waited. Tara nodded. "But, babe, you gotta lay off Malik. Seriously. He knows he messed up and he really feels like shit about it." Vincent gently placed her hands down. "Like, Tee—don't you think it's weird that he told me about it in two minutes and didn't tell you? You two were here alone for five days, Tee."

"He told you 'cause you forced it out of him."

"No, Tee. Uh-uh. That's not it." Tara was silent. "Tara, I need you to be a bit more gentle with the boy. Please. For me. He's soft, Tee."

"I know, Vincent. I know he's soft."

Vincent exhaled loudly. He shook his head.

"What? What?!"

"You know what."

"Fine, I'm sorry. I'm sorry okay? I just saw the way my dad got walked on—"

"Malik is not your father. Malik is Malik, Tara. Malik is only Malik."

"Okay. Okay."

• • •

Malik wrote the letter. Or rather he translated it, more or less. The words, the sentiment, were Tara's. Of course he agreed with everything his mother suggested: he *was* under the strong impression that Kevin had mistreated her that night. (They—Tara, Malik—decided mutually on the word "mistreat." They didn't want to be presumptuous.) He wrote that the possibility of her mistreatment caused him much sorrow. And Malik *did* want Sabrina to talk to him about it if she needed or wanted to. Absolutely. Everything Malik said in the letter was true. But what Malik wanted too was to have the words come from his mouth, not have Sabrina see them imprisoned—impotent— in his scratchy script. But she wasn't talking to him. Malik wasn't sure those words would arrive from him even if she were, but she wasn't. So he did as he was told. He wrote the letter and before sending it he showed it to his mother and she suggested that he include an offer to support her if she decided to pursue legal action. He rewrote the entire thing to include the revision and after closing the envelope, wrote "Private and Confidential" over the seal the way his father told him he should do. He stuck it through the grate of her locker Monday after school and walked home feeling both anxious and relieved.

Sabrina was absent from Drama the following day and Malik lied to his mother about it that same evening, claiming he himself missed class on student council business. He didn't want her to worry. She'd chilled out over the last couple days; it looked like she was over being mad at him. But still, he knew she was stressed about it and the fear rotting his belly was plenty for them both. Wednesday morning he got to school early, this time legitimately for council business. He sat with another grade rep, cutting big block letters out of construction paper for a sign they had to put up for the dance that Friday. Not naturally dexterous, Malik sat there with his back curled and his head down, concentrating totally. His colleague went to the bathroom and the quiet of the hallway was suddenly interrupted by female voices. He looked up to see a group of jersey-clad girls descending the staircase. Sabrina tailed the group, buckled over in laughter. Malik returned to his cutting, mustering the full extent of his focus. He heard the clack of cleats moving in his direction. It stopped. His nose was flooded with the smell of baby powder.

"Malik," said Sabrina and only then did he look up. She looked giant, her face glistening. "I got your letter. Thanks. But I'm okay," she said.

Malik had to think before he replied.

"Alright?" she said.

"I'm glad you're fine. I'm really really glad to hear that, Sabrina."

"I gotta run. Practice. I'll see you around." Sabrina turned around and jogged down the hall. Malik watched her go. Her cornrows were black and purple now. He took his phone out his pocket and called home. He wasn't sure who he'd hope would pick up.

Poems

Molly Peacock

Toronto

It's a lake.
It's a bridge.
It's a hunk of steel.
It's my take,
it's my hitch,
it's my evening meal.
By the lake
is my wedge
in the hyper-real
hypervision of the 21st century.

Here she wakes
by the ledge
by a brink she feels.
As a colour
as a weather,
she's metallic blue.
With the green glass of her windows
and the ruby of her Rocket
and the vendors in her markets
and the verdigris, the verdigris
the roofs of the 19th century
on a triangle building
on a spire.

She's a condo.
She's a parkette.
She's a Firkin Bar.
She's I want to.
Do you want to?
Yes, I want to.
She's Toronto.
She's the fact that
we can't fake it
since you can't fake
a mosaic.

She's New York's younger sister
in a flirty cloud-blue skirt.
She's new gold;
she's the 21st century flirt.

The blue of the water,
the grey inside the why,
the silver of complexity,
the haze of ambiguity.
the growing ache,
the price of mistakes:
a figure by the lake
bent over by the weight
of its future.

Frightened
burdened
it wants to rise
but when it looks across the century
it tries to hide its eyes.
Now it's rising
from a heap of sand
and realizing
that it's taking command.

There's a silver nativity
and a blue proclivity
at the base of the city's flame.
There's the shock of three O's in her name.
The O of her halo,
The O of surprise,
The polyglot O of the potentially wise.

Leggy Lady by the Lake

The CN Tower is supposed to be phallic,
but I just don't see her that way.
Just because she's long and metallic
doesn't mean she's a man—
two thirds up, there's a round, voluptuous band.
She's a leggy lady in a bustier.

Decision to Change

A move to Toronto

When the senses fleur—taste buds, finger tips,
a flicker in the corner of the lips—
something so quick, so low, then very slow,
something you don't even know you know
wakens a reception you don't know you have,
until you start to deny it. You might even have
to protect yourself from it, if you've been
shutting yourself off from the unseen
since childhood. But this is the real adventure
of adulthood: mere indenture to fact
finally reaches its limit and you can act
without looking, pricking your ears to the sound
no one else seems to hear through the air
            but you, all on your own.

Diaspora

I could lose you, but I haven't so far.
I might amuse you, but I daren't, so far.
I could confuse you, but I won't, so far.
Would I refuse you? *No,* I say.

I've chosen you, yes, this far
from where I was born, faraway
from where I woo you, using my hands

to soothe you, meeting your hands.
Now our fingers smooth out the view
as if we're stretching a canvas of a landscape
back onto the land itself—but too big! but too far—

we dive beneath its contours, everything blurs
then you drop a clue,
                   and the land reshapes;
I pick it up,
             and we pull through,
                  so far.

Poems
James Harbeck

Atlas, Behind the Theatre

Dumpster, Hummingbird Centre

Atlas sits on the loading dock
filled with tatters, stocky, broken,
open topped, the trash within
all that's known of business past.

Atlas greets the daily traffic
seething past the matinées
saying happiness can be dreamed
after stage and scene are trashed.

Atlas peels from red to brown,
feeds the rats around his bed,
sends to ground a plaster dream
shrouded wet in greasy canvas.

Atlas never shows the junk
when heavies, black-clad, junk the shows,
but, loaded with dust and tragic ends,
a dumpster holds the heavens, cracked.

Reading the Paper on the Subway

Hair the ruffled, windswept prairie,
nose and glasses dug and buried
in the day's facts and friction,
sex and war, covert action,
brow the furrowed, frowning field;

scarf in grain and hay and humus,
jacket wheatsheaf, frayed and fibrous,
fingers folded on the leaves
dark and smudging, pad and crease,
pants the rise and fall of hills.

Globe and Mail, the nation's bids,
front and back, ledes and ads,
rale and cough of twitching country,
mayor's rye, trader's barley,
shield for dry Canadian eyes,

how he holds it, ploughs it, reaps it,
in his grey-thatched storehouse saves it,
harvest of the broken air,
corns of talk, lost dust of days,
sifting chaff of ink and crackle.

Eyes now lifting, in his vision,
searching still to know his station,
he reflects the ache and profit
of his hours in solemn office
late returned to hollow ground.

Soon he stands and, business folding,
goes with doors and riders yielding,
ploughing under, mounting stairs,
goes to earth and then to air,
tiller of the turning times.

To the Finish

5k, Toronto Island

hot feet, boardwalk, legs blue sore
four thousand metres of panting so far
a bit of puddle spatter, a taste of salt spray
from hungry waves or the streaming body
running ahead, follow, thirst
now less than a thousand metres to go
boards riffling, crazing the eyes
each step cracking like aching joy
each breath a lust from the stomach
hoo, hoo, HAH, hoo, hoo, HAAH, ho
now nine hundred, now eight hundred
closing on body, white shirt, go past
a blue shirt slips by merely, but no
hold it, keep it, iron and acid
in body and water on boards, *don't slip*
and five hundred metres now left
and it darkens below and is harder
and a line and people, shouts
a tree, a tree, another tree, grass
to curl up and lie on, *stop, please stop*
but *hoo, hoo, HAH, ho*
just sixty seconds now, less
gain no one else, admit no one more
when like a dream she overtakes you
yearning for the end like a lost baby
like reaching for her child in the taunting waves
nothing to do but follow her pull
go harder than you even can, burning

the greensward underfoot rolling, pitching
there is a space between the trees, and fifty
forty, *hoo, HAH,* thirty, grass
the banner, the sign, the clock
the time has all leaked out
and there's just one second more, five metres
the length of three of her in a breath
and she is there, stumble stopped, gasping, coughing up
and you steam and shake and you have both prevailed
and the rest will fall in behind
but she has her metal, her ribbon
her shiny baby, and you have your time
three strides, three lengths of a body
a breath behind, and nothing you can hold

If You Only Knew
Judy Fong Bates

An excerpt from a work in progress

71

TONY

Tony Wong smiled back at the waitress in the doughnut shop, took one final drag of his cigarette, then mashed the butt into the ash tray. He picked up his mug of coffee and gulped down the last mouthful before nodding goodbye to the still smiling waitress. The previous six months of his life had been smoke-free, but now that he was about to start teaching again he had surrendered, lighting up one, just this one to calm my nerves, he had told himself. But one became another and another. He might as well have never stopped. The resumption of his old habit was a mixed blessing. Along with the pleasure, every flick of the lighter pricked a layer of self-loathing that lurked underneath his smooth exterior, this capitulation another sign of weakness. So he reminded himself that once his nerves settled, once he got a handle on things, he would stop for good, this being only a temporary setback. There was nothing to worry about, he told himself. Damn it, he was a seasoned teacher with more than ten years' experience. It was just that he hadn't been inside a school since three years ago in Calgary. Did he still have it? The confidence that came with a capital "C"? The kind that allowed a person to control a class full of unruly kids, without resorting to being a bully. It was uncanny how they were able to sniff out insecurity and hound a teacher out of a classroom, like a herd of animals lured by the scent of blood, circling in for the kill.

Most shops on the street were still closed, the green grocers only starting to set up their outdoor displays of harvest vegetables. The pavement was already exuding heat—it was going to be a September scorcher, not the best way to start the school year. Tony stood on the sidewalk and looked up and down the near-empty street. He had been in Toronto for only three months and already he had landed a job teaching in an elementary school. Before that he had been in Vancouver for two years with Angela, neither one of them with a serious job—waiting on tables, working at a bookstore. And before that—Calgary, where life had been perfection: successful teaching careers, a home nestled in the woods of Bragg Creek. Everything was Angela's fault. What was the matter with her? Why did she have to ruin everything? His parents had been shocked by their decision to give up their jobs and leave for Vancouver. In the face of their protests Tony had muttered something about need for a change, that he and Angela wanted a new challenge in their lives. Of course they wouldn't have understood the real reason, a secret submerged deep inside Tony's very being, a secret that, if exposed, would threaten the very life he had so carefully constructed. But the news of his recent separation had scandalized his parents. And in his head he could hear his mother's voice, squawking like a parrot's, blaming Angela for everything, telling him over and over that if only he had married a Chinese girl, none of this would be happening; instead he would still be teaching in Calgary, probably the principal of a school and most definitely a father with at least one son. On one level they were right. Maybe a good Chinese girl would have stuck it out with him. Throughout his mother's hectoring, he had remained silent, unable to look her in the eye, never uttering a single word in Angela's defence. Tony knew that his parents had interpreted his behaviour as tacit agreement, perhaps even filial piety; but underneath his calm exterior he felt only self-contempt, unable to staunch the ooze of cowardice that seeped into the marrow of his bones.

As a teenager Tony had always been shy around girls. He liked to tell people about once being asked to a Sadie Hawkins dance in high school by a girl in his class. "I was caught so off guard. You see, I'd never been out with a girl before. I hadn't given the whole dating thing much thought. It was only later that I realized what nerve she must have worked up to ask me. I felt bad about it for days. I could never look her in the eye again, and yet before that we had been friendly. We had lockers next to each other and we used to joke and laugh. I was so stupid...I had no idea that she might have a crush on me. I was socially quite slow and awkward, you know. It took me a long time to get initiated. I was nineteen before I even had sex. A fear of intimacy, I suppose," he would say with a wry smile, his tone self-deprecating, yet light-hearted.

But Angela was different, Tony told people. She had caught him off balance and had smiled her way into his life. Their marriage was the stuff of fairy tales; they were smart, stylish, good-looking, a sensitive balance of togetherness and independence. They went to concerts, art galleries and fine restaurants and travelled to Europe for summer holidays. At the same time they understood each other's desire to be alone, the need for separate vacations. He was a romantic; he never forgot Angela's birthday; he made a point of surprising her with flowers when there was no occasion. Without ever voicing it, though, Tony had known deep in his heart, right from the very beginning, that it was inevitable Angela would one day leave him, that in the end he would not be able to deliver what she really wanted and that his particular brand of love and charm would not be enough to make her stay. In the past whenever this truth struck him, he felt a rush of fear, wanted to put his arms around his wife and make her promise that they, the perfect couple, would always be together.

Men found Angela irresistible, at least according to Tony. He loved to tell people about a particular incident early in their marriage when they were sharing an apartment above a store in downtown Calgary. Angela had stepped outside to wait for him. It was a hot summer day and the second floor was sweltering. She was wearing a sundress with spaghetti straps, her dark, unruly hair clumped in a loose knot on her head. When he came out of the apartment he found Angela chatting and laughing with a fellow who had pulled up in a sports car convertible with the top down, leaning toward the passenger door, obviously trying to pick up his wife. He still remembered the look on the guy's face as he watched Tony take Angela by the elbow, gently steering her away, calling her darling. That wasn't the first time; there would be others. But for some reason that moment—the shrug of her shoulders and the open-mouth smile on her face, the thin lime-green straps against her smooth, tanned skin—that particular triumph remained clear in his memory.

Angela was not classically good-looking. Her mouth was too wide, and her nose too large, Tony had always felt. What she had though was flair, something even rarer than beauty itself. It was her uncanny ability to arrange things, whether they be clothes, furniture or flowers, always arriving at a style that was unique yet timeless and that made people (and women who were better looking) notice and feel envious.

It gave Tony special pleasure to refer to Angela as "my wife," that word wife gently blowing through the circle formed by his lips. He had begged Angela to stay, to not destroy this carefully crafted life they had created as a couple. Earlier in the week there had been a letter from her, telling him that she was now living with another man. She wanted to tell him all about it, she wrote in her spidery script, how wonderful life was as a couple, that he should try

it again. By the time he finished reading the letter he was so angry that he
tore it into shreds. How dare she write to him in that gushy language,
so damn condescending, as if he had no understanding of what it was to
share a life, as if their time together somehow didn't count, that it was less
than what she was now experiencing. As if he had chosen to live alone.
For a moment longer he stood outside the doughnut shop, his jaw clenched,
thoughts of Angela racing around in his brain. He took a deep breath of hot,
humid air and stepped onto the road, dodging cars, then turned a corner
and walked down the street to Dunedin Public School where he would begin
his new teaching job.

LUCY

Lucy Peran was thirty-four years old, not quite middle-aged, but no longer
considered young. She was one of those women often described as plain,
a rather harsh assessment when it would be more accurate to say that she
was almost pretty. Her features were even, her teeth straight and skin clear,
but there was something missing, and without that whatever, the overall
impression was mousy, pinched and uptight. When she smiled her lips often
remained closed, a tight line stretching across her face.

Lucy lived alone and, since leaving her parents' home, had always lived
alone. She wasn't without friends. She went to movies and concerts with
a couple of women from work and a few years ago she had dated a man, a
rather nice man who had wanted more from her, wanted something she
knew that she would never be able to give. Her hand never felt quite right
in his, and after he kissed her, put his tongue in her mouth, she pushed the
nice man away, not aggressively, but gently, with an almost apologetic smile
on her face, and rushed into the bathroom where she bent over the sink and
cupped handfuls of water to her mouth, rinsing away his saliva.

She now resided in predictable solitude in a leafy residential neighbourhood of Toronto, in a two-bedroom apartment on the third floor of a
yellow-brick, fifties-style, low-rise condominium. It had taken her a long
time to find the right place. She didn't want to buy into a complex that was
too large, where she would be separated from strangers (whose intent might
be questionable) by only a door and flimsy plaster walls. At the same time
she didn't want to be in a building that was too small, one of only eight or
ten units where you might become intimately aware of each other's comings
and goings. This find was perfect: six stories with forty-eight units.

When the real estate agent first showed Lucy the building, she knew right
away that she wanted to live there. The unit that had then been for sale

was at the back with windows and a balcony overlooking a tree-filled ravine. The moment she stepped onto the balcony her mouth fell open with astonishment at the lush, green tree tops so close that she could almost touch them. She had no idea that you could live in the middle of the city and feel enveloped by such peace and seclusion. But when she stared down into the steep ravine a sudden tightness gripped her chest and the sense of wonder that she felt for this secret paradise turned to fear. She would not be able to live here. Nothing would convince her. It did not matter that the slope was near impossible to climb or that the surrounding grounds were secured by a high fence; nothing was a match for her imagination. Already she could feel the effects of sleepless nights, her body tensing at the slightest noise, hearing someone scaling the heights and climbing over her balcony, and then god knows what. Just thinking about it made her shudder and her mouth go dry. She stiffened her shoulders and, with a wry smile, told the agent that she couldn't afford "paradise." But she refused to look at another building and waited for over a year before a less expensive apartment on the third floor, facing the street, became available. The location was perfect: only two blocks from the subway station meant she would never have to sit in a taxi and be at the mercy of a stranger behind a wheel who might have hidden intentions. Being on the third floor was just right—enough distance from the ground to deter an intruder from climbing, yet not so high that she had to take the elevator and share that small enclosed space with someone she didn't know, breathing the same air, feeling queasy from the smell of a stranger's body emissions. Everything was now as it should be. Lucy had made sure of that.

Lucy stepped out of the shower, threw on her pale blue terry robe and walked onto her apartment balcony in her bare feet. Already the warmth of the sun had penetrated the concrete floor. She looked at her hanging basket of mauve petunias and picked off the dead blossoms before reaching for the watering can. After Lucy emptied the can she set it on the balcony floor and reminded herself to fill it before leaving for work. The other day she had read in a magazine that plants should never be watered directly from a tap, that the water should sit for at least three hours in order for chlorine to dissipate. Lucy leaned over her railing and looked down at the street below. She ran her fingers through her wet, matted hair and sighed. She was bone-tired and wanted to crawl back into bed, wrap the rumpled sheet around her body and bury her face in the pillow. Since mid August she had been feeling twinges of dread. It always seemed to start with a vague stiffness in her shoulders that she managed to control by swimming several lengths in the condo's pool and by walking, staying ahead of the dark cloud that would devour her should she let her guard down, if only for a moment. All she had to do, she reminded herself, was survive this first day of school; then everything would be fine.

The air was heavy with moisture and thick with the stench from the animal-rendering plants northwest of her neighbourhood—a burning acrid smell that clogged your nostrils and caught at the back of your throat. Now that school was about to start, the heat that had been absent all summer had burst all over southern Ontario. Lucy took a deep breath and went back inside her apartment. She would have to hurry if she wanted to get to school by eight o'clock. Inside her little galley kitchen she made herself a cup of clear tea and ate a slice of toast and jam, then quickly washed her dishes and put everything away before getting dressed.

By the time she left the streetcar stop and arrived at the three-storey red brick building, the skin around her neck felt sticky and her nose was shiny with perspiration. During the streetcar ride she had nodded off, but fortunately the car came to a screeching halt and startled her awake. The night before she had sipped a cup of camomile tea while she ironed her skirt and blouse, then relaxed in a soothing bath, yet she had still been plagued by fitful sleep. Every time she had felt herself descend into a dark gentle slumber, something seemed to reach down like a giant hook and jolt her back into consciousness, her body rigid and exhausted. There was no reason for her to be anxious. She had spent every day last week in her classroom preparing. Her bulletin boards were bordered with autumn scenes and cards showing examples of printing and cursive script. The desks were arranged in tidy groups of four, with three stand-alones close to her work station. Every surface in the room had been wiped clean and every plastic basin washed. She had enough work for her students to last a week. It was her eleventh year of teaching. I am a seasoned teacher, she told herself. Yet this first day of school, like all the other first days of school, started with fatigue and an uneasy stomach that even dry toast and plain tea would not quell.

Lucy stood in front of the open door to her classroom, her fingers fidget-ing with a button on her blouse. It was that moment of silent anticipation, just before the teacher on outside duty gave the signal to allow the students, who had lined up at the entrance, to enter. Already she could hear feet charging up the stairs and teacher admonitions. *Walking. Walking. Hands on the railing. Hands on the railing.*

She stood with her back straight, willing herself to stay awake. The sleep that had eluded her all night now beckoned like the arms of a lover. Yet the moment the students started to file past her, she summoned herself and shrugged off the mantle of sleep that threatened to seduce her. She greeted her grade three students with a friendly, but not eager, smile. It was important to be not too effusive. Better to start off a little distant and warm up later if the situation permitted.

She told the students to sit at whichever desk they chose. A couple of them glanced at each other, confused. Lucy smiled at herself and wondered what they might do if they knew the real reason for her flexibility. Her little gift of freedom revealed to her things about them that might otherwise take weeks to discover. The best friends, the established cliques, the leaders, the outsiders. Even eight-year-olds understood the meaning of power and position.

Dunedin Avenue was a mixed bag of a school with its population of immigrants, poor whites, middle and upper-middle class kids whose parents were gentrifying certain pockets of the neighbourhood. The only child who caught her attention that first morning was Jonas Harvor, confident and handsome with his thick dark hair and intense blue eyes. One of the things that Lucy had learned early in her teaching career was that most children under the age of ten wanted to like their teacher, were in fact eager to please. But Jonas had refused to reciprocate her smile and had glanced at her as if he saw through her: as far as he was concerned he was her equal. He wasn't openly rude and did the morning work that was assigned. But there was something about the perfunctory way in which he worked, the way he treated her authority with a certain dismissiveness that made her watchful. While he stood in line for recess, she overheard him telling other students that his father drove a Mercedes. *My dad's the boss of the computer department at the university and he knows Bill Gates. You never heard of Bill Gates!? You're such a loser. Bill Gates's the richest man in the world and you've never heard of him. He invented the computer. I hope you know what a computer is.* Here was a child who understood status and pedigree. There was such confidence in his sneer. What other child in the class would be able to stand up to that? By mid morning he had picked his satellite of friends. From that brief encounter with Jonas, Lucy, in spite of being the teacher, felt wary of this child. She could feel him looking down from his high perch at a teacher who was his social inferior.

Lucy locked the door to her classroom and made her way to the staffroom, still preoccupied with Jonas Harvor, so much so that were it not for Tony Wong's quick and fluid reaction, she would have walked straight into him and his cup of hot coffee. Tony's hand shot up and grabbed her shoulder, stopping her in her tracks. Lucy didn't like it when people touched her, especially unexpectedly. She liked it even less as she felt a sudden flush of heat in her face while Tony held her at arm's length and smiled. She found herself embarrassed by her unexpected attraction to this very handsome man, and quickly lowered her eyes. Lucy was afraid to look up. She muttered something that sounded like sorry, then quickly walked away.

For the rest of the morning her students seemed far away. There was a vague memory of them returning from recess and being assigned work. When Lucy glanced at the wall clock she realized that in another ten minutes the lunch bell would ring. She told her students to clear their desks and to line up at the door, all the while wondering if the stranger with the cup of coffee would be in the staff room. Who was he? A teacher? A parent? She could still feel the slight pressure of his hand, its residual warmth on her shoulder.

The Tangerine Conundrum

Shila Desai

It was when JD suffered a second stroke that matters came to a head in the Meerchand household. There was no way Birla could continue nursing him around the clock when she was getting frail herself. He would have to go into a nursing home.

The problem was that JD refused to go unless Birla accompanied him. Birla suspected it was a point of honour for JD to have her, his wife, accompany him to what would probably be his last repository.

Anjali, their daughter, visited several nursing homes. After long discussions with the administrator about the need for both her parents to enter the facility together, she selected the Fern Hill Long Term Care Facility in Leaside. It was housed in a modern building, adjoining a small park. On the warm April day when Anjali first visited Fern Hill, a few of its occupants were being walked or wheeled around the park by attendants in blue-grey uniforms. She tried to picture her father in one of the wheelchairs, hopefully with Birla wheeling him. It looked like a happy enough sort of place, with daffodils pushing their irrepressible cheer through the earth all over the park. Inside, lunch was being served in a light-filled dining room, with a pervading smell of boiled cabbage. Anjali resolved to bring in tiffins of curry and dhal.

It was a Tuesday morning when Birla's probable fate was revealed to her by Anjali. Birla sat at her kitchen table, peeling a tangerine for JD's breakfast.

Nursing home. Land of the living dead. And all for JD. With her fingers, she carefully removed every bit of the pith for fear that it might choke him. The flesh lay exposed, glimmering faintly, and the smell of tangerines scented the air. Her fingers crushed tiny juice-filled vesicles that released their bounty to drip from her fingers, which she normally licked off with relish. Today, it made the bile rise to her throat.

"Mamma, it'll be fine," said Anjali, stressing the "fine." "They have socials and seniors' outings and all kinds of activities." The administrator had given her a week to decide, and then the spots would go to the next two on the waiting list.

Birla continued peeling the tangerine, although the movement of her deft, practised fingers became slow and deliberate. She gave it all her attention, as though the succulent depths of the fruit held an answer to a conundrum that had long perplexed her.

Anjali leaned a little closer to her mother. "You can even continue dressing for dinner," she said. "Take your saris and evening shawls and beaded purses."

Birla looked up and past Anjali into the hallway to catch her reflection in a mirror. Her trademark streak of white hair juxtaposed against the surrounding black jumped back at her. Too Indira Gandhi. She must ask her hairdresser to tone it down the next time. Next time... she would be in the nursing home, if JD had his way.

• • •

He hadn't needed her, ever, until now. Not when he was building the business empire that was theirs no longer; not when he was travelling the world purportedly on business; and not when he took up with his floozy. Meanwhile she, Birla, had given him two sons and a daughter. She'd been a dutiful wife, mother, and daughter-in-law for most of her seventy-three years. Admittedly, their sons hardly visited, and did not offer to look after them as good Indian sons should. But that was hardly her sons' fault. Everyone knew that when sons got married these days, it was their wives who ran the show, unlike her own experience of marriage.

And now... she was being asked to follow JD, like a sati to the funeral pyre.

She had married him when she was seventeen; a raw bride, a shy, naive virgin. It was an arranged marriage, of course. In 1949, when memories of the war had begun to recede, JD sailed to his ancestral homeland in Rajasthan on the western coast of India to search for a bride from a "good family." His home was in Macau; his family owned two trading houses that supplied— smuggled?—imported ivory to the insatiable Chinese market. His father had died at an early age, and JD and his brothers had built up the business under their mother's iron hand. The Meerchands were rich and influential, and Birla's parents did not ask too many questions, as long as Comfort and Servants and Motor Cars were assured. Birla's mouth twisted in a smile as she recalled how much it had meant to her in the beginning. There were flashy parties and giddying socials—some would say social climbing—in the Indian community in Macau. Birla travelled back to India regularly with her mother- and sisters-in-law so that she could shop at boutiques that had hitherto been out of bounds. It was imperative the Meerchands were seen to wear only the best, speak only the Queen's English, be driven in Mercedes-Benzes and send their children to the finest British boarding schools. After the wedding, Birla's mother-in-law took her for a weekly etiquette lesson to a British-run school near Lotus Square to stamp out the Rajasthani intonation from her spoken English.

"And make sure she knows how to pour tea and hold a teacup before the month is out," Mrs. Meerchand Senior said to Mrs. Colbert-Rhys. "This one needs a lot of work."

Mrs. Colbert-Rhys glanced at Birla, and smiled uncomfortably. "Of course, Suneeta."

Birla had marvelled at the way Mrs. Colbert-Rhys breathed out her "of courses," as if there was never the slightest doubt of what she was "of coursing" being otherwise. Back home, Birla stood in front of a mirror in her bedroom, and practised.

• • •

On Thursday, Anjali resolved to take her parents to Fern Hill Long Term Care Facility for a visit. It might help soften Birla. After all, the efficient-looking nursing home was a step up from the dingy apartment they lived in at Dundas and Sherbourne. She took the afternoon off from her job as an archivist at Toronto Reference Library, leaving her with enough time to stop off at the home that she shared with Thomas. She had thought she would be able to go through what was likely to be an ordeal at the nursing home on her own, but at the last minute, she called Thomas at the university. He was lecturing, but was able to slip out between lectures to pick up a quick lunch for her and greet her at the door of their apartment with a long hug. A half hour later, she held on to the memory of the touch of his warm hand on her cheek as she arrived, flushed and breathless, at her parents' to help JD into his wheelchair.

At twenty-six, Anjali thought of herself as self-assured, except when she had to face her mother after being with Thomas. Always, the same thought crossed her mind: "If I could only tell Mamma about Thomas!" Thomas, whom she loved more than life itself, and who had surely been sent to her by some higher power to fill the void in her life. If Birla could only see how patiently Thomas listened to Anjali, and know that it was his counsel, clear and compassionate, that Anjali acted upon as she wrestled with the responsibility of looking after her parents' welfare.

In her parents' apartment, Anjali busied herself with unnecessary adjusting of the wheelchair controls before quickly wheeling JD to the elevators. Birla shuffled a few steps behind. In the hallway, Anjali jabbed at the elevator button and held it down for several seconds before it lit up.

"They play bridge at this place," she said to her father. She had stopped addressing him as Papa a long time ago. When she referred to him in conversation with Birla, she simply said "he" or "him." "They have a little hamster in a cage in the community room on your floor. Imagine that, you already have a pet, and you're not even there yet!"

JD looked at her intently through rheumy eyes as she talked. He seemed to digest her words slowly, weighing carefully before deciding on a response.

"Hrmmph," he said. Then he turned to Birla. "Did that scoundrel Ambrose Gidoowani ever repay those two hundred and thirty-four pounds? He took that money from me in 1957. A new car, that's what he said he needed. Why I ever gave him that money, I don't know." His speech was halting, but each syllable was enunciated clearly.

The elevator arrived with a great clanging noise. Inside, Birla's eyes met Anjali's over JD's head, and Birla rolled her eyes heavenward. Anjali gave a watery smile, and quickly looked away.

At the nursing home they were met by the administrator, a stout woman with fashionably elongated spectacles that rested precariously on her large nose. She began fielding Anjali's questions in a crisp, not unkind way. Birla noticed that Anjali worded her questions to elicit a positive response. For instance, she didn't ask why there were so many security alarms on all the doors, or why signs in the elevators announced limited access to the fifth floor.

Birla decided to take over. "What is on the fifth floor?"

"Oh, those are our long-term residents who need extra care."

They exited at the fourth floor. More cheerful signs: advising, inviting, exhorting residents to join this activity and that; drumming sessions, chess games, line dancing; trips to Casa Loma and Stratford and Niagara Falls. Anjali exclaimed over it all. A fresh pine scent masked a stale food smell, and something else that Birla could not place—stale bodies? There were long corridors fronted by waist-high brown-tinted windows that looked out into a walled-in grassy central courtyard. The day being warm, there were several residents below, some walking and others in wheelchairs. Birla watched them go round and round the courtyard.

They stopped in to say hello to the pet hamster of the fourth floor. He was trying to mount his exercise wheel, furiously clawing with dizzying speed, but getting no purchase. Outside the community room, doors leading off from the corridor had little glassed-in alcoves where the residents—or perhaps the nursing home staff—had placed mementoes of younger, more mobile days; wedding and family photos and little trinkets from vacations in faraway lands. They arrived at two doors opposite each other that stood ajar. Inside each was a hospital bed, an armchair and desk, a TV and a small closet. The coverlet on the bed was carefully coordinated with the drapes and the upholstery on the chair. The carpet was a dull blue.

Birla walked into one of the rooms and felt the walls closing in on her. Her breath shortened and her heart began beating as if she were a caged bird. She grasped the edge of the bed for balance. In the other room, she heard the administrator say, "Mr. Gilligan, he was in here for fourteen years. Never a peep out of him, he was such a sweetie, and always happy. He was over a hundred when he left us."

Fourteen years, fourteen years. The words banged around in Birla's head.

"Hundred years...I will live a hundred years. I must!" piped JD unexpectedly. He was eighty-two.

• • •

JD's father had succumbed to a heart attack, so no one was surprised when JD inherited his heart condition. However, it was balanced by his mother's longevity; she had died in her ninetieth year in Macau. That was when the family fortunes had begun to spiral downward. Still, the Meerchands were a force to be reckoned with, and at her mother-in-law's death, Birla, as the eldest daughter-in-law, unconsciously morphed into the role the old woman had held within the family. She developed a haughty air, began dying her hair so that a white swathe was left to swoop over her forehead, and stopped asking questions in case her ignorance on any matter became known.

And so, Birla did not question when JD absconded to Canada, after he inveigled the business into some shady deals and his creditors caught wind. He left behind Birla, his two sons and Anjali. Had he stayed on in Macau, he would have stood trial in a month and probably ended up in prison. Birla recalled the day he came home in the afternoon, which was so alarming in itself that it should have raised a red flag. Normally he didn't get back home till close to midnight, after an evening at the club. The club was off limits to the Meerchand women. It was where the men went to down a few whiskies and behave as badly as they wished when the alcohol had its desired effect. It was also where Birla was sure JD had met Payal, and where he carried on his nine-year affair with her.

JD yelled for his suitcase as soon as he came home that afternoon. When their houseboy got it out of the storeroom, it had a broken handle, and JD asked him to fetch Birla's red suitcase instead. He didn't ask if he could borrow it. He began packing without a word to Birla. Birla watched in silence. She assumed he was leaving on a business trip. In twenty minutes, he was on his way to the airport. He later phoned from Toronto to say he would send for them when he was able to. On the phone, he was brusque, cutting her short and not permitting any questions. She was not about to ask any.

Looking back, Birla wondered if he had kept his imminent escape from her because he was afraid she would let the word out.

The business floundered, but was propped up by the younger brothers. In time, it recovered; the scandal lost its zing and people found something else to talk about. In Birla's mind, however, the stench of shame lived on, and she felt bitter toward JD for destabilizing her world just when she was coming into her own. Her sisters-in-law began ignoring her edicts and politely excluding her from basic decisions such as when to bottle the pickle and what to cook for dinner. Birla and her children lived on the extended family's charity, for JD had not found a job yet. After eighteen months, JD sent for them, and they began their new life in Canada.

Perhaps it was the early years as poor immigrants, scraping by on filial and government handouts, that distanced her sons. Perhaps it was the western culture, all pervasive, all invading, unstoppable. Perhaps—just perhaps—she and JD had driven them away with their long silences and unvoiced accusations and disappointment with what life had thrown up at them. But Anjali had turned out differently. It may have had something to do with being the last born, having witnessed the head-on struggles her brothers had with their father, and having learned from watching and listening to avoid certain taboos that littered their lives like unexploded landmines. Birla noticed that as Anjali grew up, she did everything—homework, chores, exchange of necessary information—exactly as she was supposed to, but it was difficult to figure out what went on behind the façade.

And now this nursing home business. Birla was certain Anjali wanted Birla to accompany JD out of concern for her father. Now that they had visited the nursing home and seen it was a reasonable sort of place, they could both see that JD would do just fine on his own. In fact, Birla would tell Anjali tomorrow that she would *not* accompany JD into the nursing home. JD would be livid, but—Birla shrugged and felt a huge load lift off her. For once, she would have her way. She was sure that Anjali would not allow her to live on her own, and would eventually capitulate and invite Birla to move in with her. Anjali had always been a good daughter.

• • •

The phone rang early Monday morning in Birla and JD's apartment. Birla had finished peeling JD's tangerine and was about to serve him his breakfast. She answered the phone.

"Mrs. Meerchand, my name is Thomas Kirkey."

Birla thought it was a telemarketer and was about to hang up when the man on the other end said, "You don't know me, but I know your daughter. It's about Anjali."

JD was looking intently at Birla. She turned her back to him and walked away slowly to the other room, as she had done in the past when Anjali, as a teenager, wanted to go out with her friends and JD, had he known, would have forbidden it. Mother and daughter would share an unspoken signal and retreat, one after another, away from JD. Birla would listen to Anjali's request and acquiesce, even as she wondered what she would tell JD.

The man continued, "We have been seeing each other for the past two years. In fact we are living with each other. We want to marry." There was a pause. "With your and Mr. Meerchand's blessings."

Birla stood looking at dust particles in the stream of early morning sunshine that coursed in through the window. There was really that much dust in the air, and she had never noticed it.

The man's voice resonated in the silence that followed. It was even and pleasantly modulated, with a slight West Indian accent that prominently rounded out the vowels. Living with each other? Did that mean what she thought it meant?

"Does Anjali know you are calling me?"

"No, Mrs. Meerchand, I'm afraid not." He cleared his throat. "She has wanted to tell you, but hasn't been able to. I think she's afraid you won't understand. She hasn't been sleeping well, and is upset about you having to go into a nursing home with Mr. Meerchand. She says you do not need to go, but..."

"But I have no choice," said Birla.

"That's what I am calling you about. We would like you to come live with us."

Birla felt her knees buckle, and she groped behind her for a chair to sink into. She was breathing heavily now. Even as she told herself not to make a fool of herself with this polite young man on the other end of the line, a vista opened up in front of Birla's eyes. An economical but tasteful wedding, life together with Anjali and this nice young man, the grandchildren that were sure to follow, and whom she would take to visit JD, safely ensconced in the nursing home...

His voice brought her back. "I have to mention something," he was saying. "I am not Indian. I am black."

Birla closed her eyes and breathed deeply to slow the thumping of her heart. Her hand gripped the chair handle. She thought she wheezed a little but finally found her voice.

"I have a few questions." She paused. "Do you make my daughter happy? Does she love you? Does she laugh with you?" She was surprised as the questions tumbled out, as though they were once-beloved but long-forgotten pressed flowers floating out from between the pages of a book that was suddenly upended on its spine.

"Yes." His reply was instant, confident. "We laugh together all the time."

• • •

It was late before Birla cleared away the remnants of dinner and helped JD into bed. After, she laid out the tangerines on the kitchen table for tomorrow's breakfast. Tomorrow, Anjali would come in the morning for a discussion of their plans. Then, she was to call the administrator at Fern Hill with their final decision.

He—Thomas—was black. A black man and her daughter. They were living together. How would she ever face the world? From inside her, a voice mocked—what world? Who cared? In Macau, people would have talked and she would have lived with shame. But this was Canada, this was the new world. Thomas had said Anjali laughed with him. Birla couldn't remember Anjali laughing much with either her or JD. Had she, Birla, ever laughed with JD? She was laying out the cutlery beside the breakfast dishes when the fork she was holding clattered over JD's setting. She sat down heavily. She couldn't remember ever laughing with JD.

Early the next morning, Birla got down her red suitcase, the same one that JD had packed when he left Macau for Canada. She got out her saris and evening shawls and beaded purses and began neatly packing them into the suitcase.

Poems
Barbara Hunt

Giengener Tanz (the dance)

He was their yenta
say some old Jews
of Hitler who scattered them

yet threw them into close embrace.
My parents at ten were flotsam too.
Mama, caught on the sidelines

watched the starlit bombing runs
splash someone else's sky
in lieu of blackened movie screens.

Lives rationed. She cut men's suits down
for women left behind.
Papa yielded his childhood Litau'vich years

DPed in Prussia and Poland,
far from the home farm
—only at seventeen to outrun

iron borders refashioned by Russians tanks
until some small town dance
found him, by chance

up against the cheek,
of one whom he'd crossed continents
to marry.

The Beaverbrae

(refugee ship sailing from Germany to Canada after World War Two)

Orphaned, around the world you sail
your ship of hope, a blackened scow
men muttering in darkness, babies wail.

Mothers, grandmothers dipping bale
-ful crusts in strongest tea allowed.
Orphaned, around the world you sail

slung in stacked coffins, you're availed
some snatch of sleep up in the prow
men muttering in darkness. Babies wail

their cries piercing your drifting veil
of dreams—your cardboard bag in tow.
Orphaned, around the world you sail

and sliding into Union, ride the rail
of hopes hanging like socks 'cross rooming-house row
men muttering on Markham, babies wail

no more. With hammer, trowel, you cannot fail.
Sweat buys a purchase in land of milk and money, so
ignore men muttering and babies' wail
as, orphaned, around the world you've sailed.

Benalto Road

Words were breadcrumbs
no one could pick up
they soured on her tongue
as round and round

the Ukrainian bakery, the Yiddish deli, the chinaman...
At night she fell on phrases by feeble lamplight
nibbled foreign fare by book and
gummed them like a teething tot.

He'd sent for her
a parcel shipped as *cargo*
her cardboard case of school girl dreams
no match for all the boot-factory stares

riding that corrugated King-car.
No refuge in that crackerbox
stacked with his cousins, wives
whose sharp, reheated arguing ate air

and he, the only wordless one...
So she found solace in the park
wide open green soothed summer's blister
winter's bluster, a shock-cold slap

like those lunatics she now called *family.*
Come January she'd grown that new life deep inside,
no fleeing on hidden feet, no passage back,
her taut-skinned belly bore it out.

She coveted all that her raw hands could clasp.
And in the end, a judge decreed
that she should call Benalto home
because her husband and new daughter did.

Armadillo

Clara Ho

Connie cries for hours, the tears welling up. She's an endless fountain and the words that I offer are not the least bit effective in making her stop.

I feel like I am really not here while she is doing this: breaking up and down. I make the necessary gestures, go through the motions that someone in my position should—a touch on the shoulder, a reaching out for her hand—but really, my actions are all orchestrated, rehearsed even, as I have been through this thousands of times before. My sister, the drama queen. She has the uncanny ability to think only of herself, particularly at times of extreme distress and emotion. I contemplate whether my presence is actually of any comfort to Connie. If I ran out to get a coffee would she even notice?

"I have to work in the morning. Early." I try to emphasize the word "early." I get up and hope that I can make my way to the door without any objections from Connie.

"Don't go." Connie says, as she continues to sob. I try to avoid the balls of tissue strewn across her living room floor. She whimpers quietly and I find myself rooted in place. I make the mistake of turning around and looking at her.

I succumb to her pleading eyes and her sad expression. A look she has mastered since our childhood and that I am all too familiar with. Once again, she has triumphed and I agree to stay the night on her small loveseat, a chair really. It's cherry red with chrome legs and is more fashionable than functional. Definitely not meant to be slept on unless you have four legs, purr a lot and cough up the occasional hairball.

Connie's snoring from the next room keeps me awake. She has cried herself into a deep sleep. Wish I had done the same.

I will regret this in the morning. I know that my body will ache and I will be too tired for the meeting that I have with Mr. Whitaker, the difficult client I was saddled with because I was away the week the others at the office divvied up the work.

Lucky me.

• • •

Five months later, I find myself comforting Connie again in her apartment. She is at the end of yet *another* epic love affair.

She goes through these patterns just as I do not. She meets some guy, dates him for a while, convinces herself that he is indeed "the one." There have been so many "the ones" that I have long lost count. I can usually tell early on when it is not going to work. Ma sees the signs too. We both choose not to say anything to Connie and are in silent agreement that nothing we say would matter. My sister would not heed our warnings no matter how well intentioned.

Then, just as quickly as it begins, it ends: first the anger, then the crying, then the resentment. All vocalized clearly and in a way that makes my parents question sometimes whether they actually gave birth to Connie. When I was five years old I would tell people at school that my baby sister was adopted. If it weren't for our striking resemblance, I would be inclined to stick to my story still.

Hiding behind his newspapers, my father takes the reserved position. He sits in his old mustard-coloured recliner in the corner, flipping slowly through the pages of his papers. You'd be amazed at how many Chinese newspapers one can purchase. My sister and I arrive at my parents' house for our weekly Sunday evening family dinner. My father does not even look up when we arrive.

Ma comes to the door in her floral apron, her hands still wet from having just washed them. She greets us carrying a plate of oranges sliced into wedges. She thrusts the plate at us as she herds my sister and me toward the sofa. She sits with us for a few minutes before she returns to the kitchen to finish preparing dinner.

With dinner my mother will try to smother Connie's heartbreak with an array of specially prepared dishes. The many soups and herbal concoctions she will conjure up are meant to bring good luck and good fortune if you eat them. Long life. Prosperity. Love even. She will present them to Connie but they'll go unnoticed. Connie is a picky eater and this breaks my mother's heart, though she will never admit it.

The aromas wafting from the kitchen call to me. Mostly, Connie and I are not allowed to enter the kitchen unless we make it clear to Ma that we are there only to observe and absorb, not to interfere. I suspect that my mother is hiding under a cloud of secrecy in the kitchen, trying to create that special dish that will bring my sister and me health, wealth, a good-looking Chinese husband and, of course, grandchildren—lots of them. Perhaps Connie and I always knew this was what Ma was doing as she worked her culinary magic. But we resisted her attempts to teach us how to cook, how to make real Chinese food. And now we find ourselves forever banned, our exile permanent.

My mother flits in and out of the kitchen. I can tell from the way she looks at me that I am not doing enough to comfort Connie. That is my role in this family. Comforter. Like a big fluffy blanket that can make all our problems go away.

"Connie, I'm not sure John is the one." I venture.

"His name isn't John, it's Jimmy. And I love him!" Connie sobs, letting out another loud wail. She's trying to breathe and finding it difficult because she is now so congested.

"But you've only known him for two months!" I exclaim, louder than I intend to. Connie shoots me a nasty glare and I quickly realize I've said the wrong thing.

"What do you know about love?" She keeps her gaze fixed on me as she reaches for the tissues. I squirm uncomfortably as she continues to glower at me through her puffy red eyes. I reach out to pat her hand but the gesture is awkward. Connie takes her hand away, reaching for another tissue. Luckily, my parents have been stockpiling. We'll never run out. My mother can make boxes of tissues magically appear.

Nothing. I know absolutely nothing about love. Can't say I've been there before or done that in any sort of way. Having witnessed all of my sister's "love affairs," I don't feel like I'm missing much.

"You deserve better," I say. My words sound hollow and I am unable to convince myself of what I am speaking. Connie looks away and ignores me.

I want to say something else to my sister but am at a loss for words. Having grown up in a household where silence was the most common form of communication, I am amazed that I can even carry a conversation, let alone console my sister at her time of distress. I remain silent, thinking about what to say next. Ma reappears and looks at me for a moment. We both know that in a few hours, Connie will pull herself together and we will all pretend that my sister's display of emotion never happened.

The appearance of harmony is always restored in my family.

• • •

On my way back to Toronto from Vancouver following a weekend of horrendous back-to-back-to-front-to-sideways meetings, I find myself stuck on a full flight. There's no elbow room and I am wedged between two people.

To my right sits a man in his mid thirties. I can sense his potential to be chatty. He's just waiting for the cue, waiting to be spoken to and then he'll be off. I avoid saying anything, not making eye contact. He gets the window seat and that allows him to hide his anxiety by staring out the window pretending to admire the scenery. He fixates on a mysterious stain on the front of his shirt and tries to get it off. I turn away, trying to pretend he's not there.

On my left is someone entirely different.

What can I say about the woman who ends up sitting to the left of me? Only that she arrives on the plane after everyone else has been seated for about fifteen minutes without the slightest sign of concern that she has made us all wait on the runway. She's stunning and I cannot help but steal glances at her, afraid that she'll catch me staring. Just as she is about to lift her heavy carry-on into the overhead bin, several male passengers jump to her assistance as I do. But she does not need the help and everyone sits down, sheepish and embarrassed. The woman takes the seat next to me and I can feel my heart pounding as she asks me to hold her bottle of water while she rifles in her bag for some gum. I feel the envious stares of everyone around me and try my hardest to ignore them.

"Do you want a piece?" she holds out the pack of gum and for some reason I am speechless. I decline, shaking my head, unable to say a word or look her in the eyes.

About twenty minutes into the flight she falls asleep and leans toward me. I try to lean the other way but that means I am closer to the man on my right than I want to be. I succumb to the fact that I'm trapped. She rests her head comfortably on my shoulder as I sit, cramped and feeling my muscles about to seize up. I'm afraid to move in case I wake her.

I notice that she is wearing dark-framed glasses and her hair is shoulder length, slightly wavy. She's Asian, possibly Chinese. I stare at the top of her head. Throughout the flight I catch myself stealing glimpses and try to look away. Her hair smells like flowers or some sort of fruit. I want to touch it but I banish the thought quickly and try as carefully as I can to shift my body so I am slightly less uncomfortable. My efforts, however, are futile.

The plane descends and we are half an hour later than our ETA. The flight attendant wakes her.

She yawns, stretches, cat-like. She opens her eyes and looks at me. "Have I been leaning on you the whole time?"

I try my best not to look completely stiff and uncomfortable. I try to extend my arm. My shoulder cracks loudly. "It's okay. I hope you slept well."

"I'm so sorry," she apologizes. "That was a long flight too." She dazzles me with a most nonchalant smile.

"I'm Catherine." She holds one hand out as she tries to put her shoulder bag over the other arm.

I look at her hand for a moment. I reach out to take it, knowing full well even before I touch her skin that it is too late. I am hopelessly smitten and past the point of no return.

• • •

Catherine grabs her bag from the overhead bin and moves into the aisle. I wrestle with my seatbelt. A woman two rows ahead cuts in front of me as I am trying to leave the plane. She drags a small child in one hand while trying to wheel her carry-on with the other. I can see Catherine ahead of me and I cannot tell whether she is waiting or not as she hangs back at the right moments but then moves ahead. I try my best not to lose sight of her and tell myself that even if I do I will see her when I collect my luggage.

I arrive at the carousel and look for Catherine. I notice her immediately, standing where it is less crowded. I make my way to her and we wait. She does not look in my direction but I sense that she knows that I am next to her. I crane my neck, hoping that my bag does not arrive, strangely wishing that my luggage has been lost. When my bag appears I ignore it. Discreetly, I watch it ride the carousel four times before I actually grab it. I want to prolong this moment with her.

"You know, that bag has been around a few times." She gestures at my suitcase.

"Oh, really?" I try to pretend that I haven't a clue about what she is saying. I am relieved that she has finally said something to me. She laughs at the expression on my face.

"You're a horrible liar."

We head toward the taxi stand and I begin to feel desperate that there are no more opportunities for me to continue our exchange. The air is hot and I cannot seem to shake that airplane smell. I feel slightly nauseous but try my best to hide it by speaking louder than I normally would. I am oblivious to how foolishly I am behaving. We join the lineup for taxis.

"So where are you going?" I ask her. I shock myself. A sudden burst of boldness.

"Home," she pauses. "I live in the west end. In Parkdale."

"Oh, me too," I lie.

"Where exactly do you live?" she asks, suspicious, as I help her get her bags into the trunk of the taxi. "After that luggage carousel incident, I'm not sure about you." She eyes me, skeptically.

"I'll tell you someday," I say to her.

• • •

"They saw you the other day," my mother says. She's frantically making dumplings. Her hands work quickly. She has enlisted my help and that is how I know she wants to talk to me about something. I've never had a meaningful conversation with my mother unless it is about, around or related to food. The kitchen counters are cluttered with bowls and plates of mysterious ingredients. I poke my nose in each of the bowls, trying to identify their contents.

"Who saw me?" I'm confused. My mother is skilled at the art of being vague. It's genetic. I can do it too but try not to. Thousands of dollars of therapy were supposed to have cured me of this. Ma and I can have a conversation about something for hours without either of us ever stating what that "something" is. Since she is far more skilled than I am, at the end of our conversations I'm often the one who is left feeling confused.

"Auntie June and Auntie Lin." She focuses on one particularly errant dumpling that insists on spilling its contents out of its wrapper. I can tell it's one of mine. I usually try to stuff them as full as possible so we can finish faster. "In Chinatown. At the Chinese restaurant."

There are only close to a hundred Chinese restaurants in Chinatown and I am tempted to make a sarcastic comment. For my own sake, I hold my tongue. I try to balance being vague and being annoyed. I wish my mother would vocalize her disapproval. This is an attempt, on her part, to pick a fight although I know she won't actually engage in an argument with me. It's the disapproving silence that gets me every time.

"What day was this?" I play along, trying not to give anything away. I know exactly what restaurant my mother means. I grab another dumpling wrapper gruffly, stuffing a heaping tablespoon of filling onto it before I close the edges. I put the dumpling on the finished plate and watch as it spills open at the sides.

My mother has met Catherine. My father has met her too, although he looked at her for all of five seconds and then hid behind his newspaper until we ate dinner in the dining room—which was something new. Growing up, we were only allowed to eat in the kitchen. My mother would dust the dining room table religiously every week, making sure it was spotless.

During dinner my father stared intently at the dishes on the table, pausing only to put food in his mouth, breathe, slurp soup and ask practical questions of Catherine. At some point, he might have chewed as well. When he spoke, he did not look at her but only at his bowl.

"How much money do you make?" He asked her between bites without making any eye contact.

I was utterly, thoroughly, embarrassed. I wracked my brain to think of a plausible excuse for hiding under the table.

Catherine paused for a moment. She glanced over at me and I could see the slightest hint of a smile at the corner of her lips. I was too shocked to say anything at all.

"I make a pretty good living. I bought a house recently."

My dad stopped chomping for a moment and looked at me, "Look, even your friend knows that equity is good! For years I've been telling her to buy property." He kept his gaze on me as he said this and then returned to focusing on the rice in his bowl.

And now this: the dumpling inquisition. I had a conversation with my mother over the phone a week before and clarified for her three times that Catherine was not my roommate. She was, indeed, my girlfriend.

I'm certain she knew what that meant but had chosen to deny it. She moved quickly on to the next topic. I thought it was progress enough.

"Tell her to come for dinner next weekend," my mother says quickly, as she rewraps my horribly constructed dumpling. She whisks the full plate away. With that, I know that our conversation is over.

• • •

"Are you planning to not hold my hand the entire evening?" Catherine laughs. "Do you think I should hug your dad?"

The look on my face indicates my level of mortification. I can't imagine someone being closer than a foot away from my father. Even that would be more of an infringement into his personal space than he could possibly handle.

She is being playful. I can tell she wants to cause trouble but won't because she loves me too much and realizes exactly how terrified I am. She'll pretend to be my roommate and I'll dislike every minute of this as we have to watch Connie and her new boyfriend be smoochy the entire time.

"Just relax," I say to her. I take deep breaths.

Catherine stands behind me, wraps her arms around my waist and winks at my reflection in the mirror. I push her gently away so that I can check what must be the tenth outfit I have tried.

"I don't know why I'm so nervous." I take another deep breath. "We've had dinner with my parents dozens of times."

"But this is different," she pauses. "This is New Year's. Lunar New Year's eve. The time to be with family, right?"

It can't mean that much that my parents have invited her. My partner. I can't let it mean too much in case it all goes to hell. I desperately want to drink something alcoholic that will give me a strong dose of courage. But that would be an illusion really. And unfortunately, there isn't a glass in the world big enough to fit the amount of courage I need.

• • •

It's more complicated than just simply being difficult. It's a struggle that I cannot explain.

Three years into my relationship with Catherine, we decide to separate. I am heartbroken. I call Connie and she comes to my apartment and I make her sleep on my uncomfortable chair for the very first time. She does it without complaining, without saying anything, and I love her for it.

I visit my parents a few days later. They sense that something is wrong but the show of emotion that Connie can pull off just will not work for me. I can't vent and cry. Tissue boxes will not magically appear. I sit in our family room, on the same sofa that I have sat on countless times as a child and then a teenager. The sofa looks almost new as my parents insist on placing a plastic cover over it—to protect it they always used to say. I look at the photos of my family on vacation, at Connie's graduation, at my grandmother's eightieth birthday party, and they paint a picture that is not entirely true. We are not the happy family that the photos make us out to be. At least, I don't believe we are.

My parents don't know how much Catherine really means to me. They never have. Or even if they had some inkling they have never let on. They are not surprised that I have shown up to dinner alone. There are moments when I wish that they would ask about her, about why she no longer comes to dinner. Yet I'm certain that if they did ask I wouldn't know how to respond. In some ways, I am just as afraid of the truth as my parents are, except I know that I fear her absence above anything else.

I take comfort in my parent's ability to see and not see the things that are convenient, painful, a part of life. The things that they might not like so much and that we definitely do not agree on. Selective listening. Selective observation. Because they don't ask, I can play along and pretend that nothing is different. I have not been hurt or wounded. I cannot possibly feel any loss.

I hide behind my armour to nurse my wounds.

My mother has made my favourite dishes. She has made the special ginseng and chicken soup that takes all day to prepare. She puts a plate of snow pea shoots with garlic in front of me. It is perfectly cooked. And finally, she brings out the crab in ginger and onions. I know that my mother has been working all day on this meal and I wish I could be more appreciative.

She places the dishes in front of me and I make an effort to eat. I grab a tender snow pea shoot with my chopsticks and place it in my mouth. It tastes bland but I know it could not possibly be. These dishes cannot console me like her words, any of her words, could. I know my mother understands that something is wrong, just as I know that we will never be able to speak about it. She does not say anything but keeps my plate stacked with food. When I leave, she packs up more leftovers than usual for me to take home.

I stand at the door waiting, as I know she will not let me leave without her care packages. My mother hands me a bag full of Styrofoam containers. She stands in front of me and for a brief moment I think she is going to give me a hug. Instead, she reaches for the scraggly scarf around my neck and tucks it into my coat.

"It's okay, Ma." I say quietly. "It's not that cold."

My mother stops fussing. I touch her arm briefly. My hand lingers for a moment before I pull it away. I step outside and see my breath in the night air. The stars are surprisingly bright. The bag of leftovers pulls at my arm. I notice that it is heavier than usual. It weighs me down as I make my way home.

Poems
Monica Rosas

MS-13* in My Classroom

Blue pants, white stripes,
trace portable tattoos
into the fertile land of a teacher's psyche:

a place where crushed heads
and dismembered limbs
soak in liquid red.

The colours you wear bear a statement of the world
your ancestors were unfortunate to inherit.

A place where war has turned
Natives against Europeans,
Europeans against Natives,
Native Europeans against European Natives,

you against yourself.

Blue sky rushes alongside white clouds.
White petals caress blue waves.
Blue marbles roll over white sand.

The colours you wear bear a statement of America's aching past,
and the dislocation of your culture today.

---

*Mara Salvatrucha, MS-13 or MS or M-18, are street gangs from El Salvador that emerged
in the 1980s during the country's violent civil war.

A today here in T.O.,

a place where violence has turned
Blacks against Whites,
Latinos against Asians,
Whites against Whites,
Blacks against Blacks,
Latinos against Latinos,
Asians against Asians,

you against yourself.

White fog hugs a blue raincoat.
Blue bird nudges white snowflakes.
White ribbon curls around blue wool.

I watch you in your blue pants, white stripes,
writing down antiquated equations,
and wonder as your teacher,
"Could my blue, my white,
ever be your right?"

Emergency in Toronto

(Written while waiting in St. Joseph's Hospital emergency room)

The foreign woman next to me is crying
and her distraught toddler in tow
will be quelled by no one.

"Na nai, na nai," he whimpers
as he nervously kicks at the dirty floor.
He paces for the patient, which isn't him.
It's mommy,
because she's bleeding,
bleeding at twelve weeks, she told the nurse.

Numb to her son's hard pull,
his fingers grasping her face,
her low words sounding plaintive
rather than soothing,
her seated body sealed in stone.
An occasional sniffle
is the only show of emotion she allows herself,
eyes fixed on a sad silence.

So her baby son moans what she can't.
His wet face nestles between her legs—
tight curls peeking out under his scarlet fleece,
creating a disturbing image of a scream.

Scented Worlds

Sayeeda Jaigirdar

Sharmila sat still in a corner seat on the subway. She was on her way home from downtown. The officials in their shining towers had summoned her for a hearing after she had missed two citizenship tests in a row. She had expected to find herself before a judge. Instead, she was led to a large testing area and handed a citizenship test. It was their way of having one take the test. Silly official people! The whole thing was *sooo* easy. It disappointed her, as had many other things since she first arrived. What had she really expected of this land?

At the hearing, there was a *desi* Canadian government officer who tried to impress everyone with his brisk, efficient manner. He smelled a little of her father's Old Spice cologne. At first Sharmila thought that he was one of the assistants. But he turned out to be one of the commissioners. The judge appeared after the test and spoke to her rather kindly. There was no hint of a scent about him. The night before, her husband had urged her to study for a surprise test. He lectured her for ten minutes about the perils of failing the citizenship test. Her eight-year-old son warned her in sombre tones to pass so he could get his citizenship too. "It's not fair, Mum," he said. "If you fail, I get to fail too!" She had smiled at him and wondered how right he was.

All around her swirled smells. Smells that revealed the intricate contents of each colourful individual. Smells that had their own identity, like Canadian permanent resident cards declaring place of birth to the discerning. A woman wizened from the weather, probably fifty or more, in a multicoloured green-speckled sari, smelled of cumin, turmeric and *sambar masala*. When Sharmila looked at her, the woman looked away, her eyes like scurrying little mice. The *desi* kind of mice. The train stopped at Victoria Park. Sharmila wondered if her husband was going to be late again tonight.

A girl got on. Youngish, South East Asian looking. Perhaps she was Guyanese or Indian. Sharmila could barely detect a smell about her. She put her nose to the stale subway air and pulled in another waft of air to identify origin. The tangerine-honey dewy smells of Body Shop products mixed with the youthful essence emanating from her skin. She was probably born in Canada, fated to lose *desi* origins.

A voluptuous blonde slid into the seat next to the Indian girl. She seemed to be around thirty. Barbie doll curves. The kind *desi* men dreamt of and could never date. Sharmila once overheard two *desi* men in a bus. "These *angreezi* girls spend too much money and they want you to understand them," one said. "And they want to be seen around with you. The *desi* variety is definitely better."

However this blonde did not look like the Canadian wholesome variety. This was definitely the sensuous European kind. She had on an expensive oil-based perfume and a look of utter disdain. Sharmila could smell her dripping vanity in the heavy scent.

All the other women appeared to blend into the background and they looked away from the blonde; the men, however, stole covetous glances at her. Sharmila wondered if her husband would glance too, if he were here. The smell of their unrequited desires made the place warm and humid. The subway carriage was suddenly a lush torrid green jungle and the blonde, a rare colourful bird of paradise. Sharmila sighed.

The gift or, one could call it, the curse of her nose. Her nose translated everything she sniffed into words, images and unearthly visions. In school Sharmila's English teachers had always thought her extremely imaginative. Her family doctor in Toronto thought she might have a mild case of synaes-thesia, a rare neurological peculiarity in which one's sense perceptions blended into each other with startling results. "Not to worry," he said. "Many painters and writers who have this call it a gift."

Sharmila's station appeared at the end of the dark tunnel. Warden Station. She stepped off the subway, through the turnstiles and down the wet, slippery stairs. Everyone was running by her urgently, while she climbed down the steps, one at a time, holding the rail guard. It always appeared to her like a scene from a Bollywood movie, in which she was from another time zone, walking down the steps in slow motion, while everyone else was frantically in search of something. Sharmila seemed to have more milliseconds, more units of time, to experience things around her, many more than everyone else. She thought to herself, *"O baba!* What were they running for?"

These people were running in search of Time! There was no Time to eat, so *they* had fast food. There was no Time to spend with *their* children, so the little time was called quality time. There was little Time to do all of life's requirements, so there were time-management classes and little and big diaries that helped *them* manage Time. There was no Time to look after oneself, so *they* had creams, nips and tucks that turned back the hands of Time.

As Sharmila pushed open the door at the bottom of the stairway to the Warden Station parking lot, the frigid Toronto air brought in the warm smell of the breath of her *nani*, her maternal grandmother calling her across the light years from the inner chambers of her grandfather's bungalow on a chilly winter night in Sylhet. She was suddenly eight years old again in Bangladesh and listening to her *nani*, a retired school teacher, telling her about the meaning of Time. The tin-roof squeaked as the metal contracted in the cold. In the distant dark corners of the ancient forest, a jackal howled to his comrades.

"Aye, sona, Amar kache gumao."

"Nani, O Nani!"

Sharmila jumped up on her *nani's* lacquer-polished four-poster bed, under the cotton mosquito net. Her fair, round-faced *nani* ruffled Sharmila's plaited hair with her fragile fingers, through which blue veins showed. *Nani* was the fairest woman in the village. Sharmila often put Tibet powder on her face to become as fair as her beloved *nani*. *Nani* was wearing a soft white cotton sari for the night. She always wore saris to bed, unlike Sharmila's aunts, who were more modern and wore nightdresses.

"O, *Nani*, what will I look like when I am old? Will I look like you?"

"*Sona*, Time will beat all of us in the end. The only things that will remain are your faith, patience and good deeds, and the way you help other people to find the Truth."

"*Nani*, like the Buddha?"

"Yes, *sona*, and like all great men and women such as the Mahatma Gandhi, Sufi Shahjalal and Mother Teresa in Kolkata."

All this was too much wisdom for an eight-year-old in one night. Sharmila hugged her grandmother and went to sleep.

Sharmila was home at last. It looked *desi* with Canadian touches. There was her mother's brick-red and white *nakshikatha* embroidery on the wall. The elephants and the Bengali peasants in the picture bowed to her as she entered. "Asho Amar ghore asho, Amar ghore." Welcome to my home.

Her plants emitted warmth and a friendly green odour that told her how joyous they felt at her return. These were her beloved money plants, bought from the Dominion stores. She brushed their rubbery surface with a light caressing touch. Perhaps they would usher in prosperity and wealth in this new land.

Sharmila twirled around the brown carpet, touched the sand-coloured harmonium with musical reverence and then ran into her bedroom. There was an absence of anything electronic in her bedroom. Her husband had declared, a long time ago: "No television, no telephone, *kishu na*—only me and you."

In the beginning of the marriage, when they went to bed, he would not let her face any other way except toward him. And look at him she did, the dutiful obedient wife. Pretending a bit now and then. O, the endless dramas between man and wife and how they changed with the passage of time! There were times during her pregnancies when she could not bear the brutal male smell of him. Only when her children were born was she allowed to turn the other way.

She made sure that her babies were breastfed. As she lay in bed feeding one or the other, he lay on the other side, smelling her neck, waiting, on cold Toronto nights; she had often thought that heaven could not come closer than this. It was the freezing sleet on the windows outside and the warmth of the *desi* Tantric within. Even the angels would envy her...in the frosty heavens with their *hurs* and *porees*. The warm tantalizing mist of the humidifier took on the various manifestations of their desires, shaping them at will, at times intense, at times sleepily tranquil.

Perhaps this was one of the Truths that her *nani* had spoken of. People got married to keep themselves toast-warm on bone-chilly nights and also to keep out the great smothering Darkness.

Once, on a cold, frosty night, she had come face to face with a homeless person in downtown Toronto. *A homeless woman! In Canada?* She had been shocked, horrified! The odour of the homeless woman was overpowering. It twisted like an angry red cobra through her nostrils, flaring her insides. Suppose she became like one of them. It was too easy, too easy. Suppose her husband lost his job or became disabled? Or even abandoned her? Oh, why was she so afraid of being alone here? She pictured herself on a desolate Canadian landscape, with the cry of imaginary black winged birds in the greying distance.

Desi trembling heart on the cold shivering northern rocks. It was winter. Downtown Toronto. Slush, swoosh, slush and swoosh. She was begging on the streets. Shame, shame, shame, shame. She didn't know how she got there. Her feet were swollen; there was grey in her hair. Where did the grey come from? She remembered a shelter, some desi drug-dealing friends and then the streets. *She was too old for anything else. Some of the Christmas shoppers gave her some coins out of occasional pity; most just passed her by. Christmas eyes glazed with shopping lists, shopping lists, shopping lists. Some desi corporate people walked by with their white friends. Stolid butterflies in down-filled cocoons. She wanted to yell,* Look at me! I was just like you! I was just like you! I was just like you!

A Canadian winter night. A clean sweep of sparkling snow. Grey streets lined in white chalk.

The whispering lingering white fear.

The dark silent promise of a terrifying, easy death.

A crystallized white corpse in the morning downtown streets.

A fragile unborn butterfly in a chrysalis.

It was that easy. It was that easy.

Sharmila shuddered at her own fantasies. Why did she feel things so intensely? She shook her head to chase them out, like errant children, out and away from the inner chambers of her mind.

Sharmila walked up to her closet and looked at her collection of delightful, maddening saris. They were her pride and joyous past-time. She loved to touch them, to caress them, putting one melodious colourful sari against her, then another. The smell of her saris took her back to a golden age when leisure time was spent reading and listening to classics on *Nani*'s gramophone. There were the cotton *Kota* saris, the *Tangail* thread work saris, the *Rajshahi* silks, the *Mirpur Kathans* and the ubiquitous *Jamdani!* The saris spoke lovingly to her in Bengali and they made her want to sing and dance. She took out a *Jamdani* sari, eggshell white with crimson touches. Would she be daring and sport a sleeveless blouse with it? What would her husband say? Would his eyes bear down on her and be captivated all over again, or would he frown and say: *"Ki?* What's happening—you look too revealing!"

When she wore a sleeveless top with her Canadian clothes, he didn't mind "But with a *sari? Na, baba,* better not risk it."

Sharmila wished that she possessed a sari that had the magical colours of the lights and the half-lights of an Indo-Aryan dawn. One that she could drape herself with and he could gaze and gaze...She would tie him forever within the gentle waves of the cloth. But for now, she had to be content with this sari.

Sooo, would he notice this sari on her or will he not? Or would the Torontonian tiredness be in his eyes? The tiredness of the mortgage due date and credit card bills, the tiredness of yelling at children who thought nothing of their immigrant parents, the tiredness of shovelling snow, the tiredness of the slavish corporate job where a human being was told what to do and how to perform.

Before they came to this country of cold rocks, they would read poetry to each other, sometimes soothing Tagore, sometimes fiery Nazrul. Now all those poems had become icy dangling modifiers, syntactic structures that were unpronounceable tongue twisters in the northern hemisphere. A long time ago, they would sit on their veranda in the Circuit house in Bally Road and gaze with devotion at the full moon. Only a true-blooded Bengali knew the art of Gazing at the Full Moon. A book of poems would complete this sacred occasion, when the man would gaze into his consort's eyes and recite mournful verses all designed to urge the woman to swoon in *rosogollah* delight. There was more romance than lust in Bengali poems, so the end would be muted, subdued and remarkably tranquil.

It was time for her to start cooking. Out came a Bengali cookbook. Her aunt had given her this book when she had got married and set up house. "This is for you, so that your husband doesn't starve to death." They all cared more about her husband than her. No one had ever given *him* a book about anything. Yesterday, her husband had demanded a *desi* dish, so she decided to give it a try. *Potoler dolma.* It was a vegetable dish stuffed with Canadian halal minced meat.

She had gone to the *desi* shop on the corner of Markham and Eglinton yesterday. The sign proclaimed proudly: HALAL BANGLADESHI, PAKISTANI, INDIAN MEEAT SOLD HERE. Sharmila looked closely at the sentence structure. There were sudden splashes of hot red colour bursting all over her mind. Images of the bloodbaths of the War of 1971 in Bangladesh flashed by like a silent movie. It was like watching a bioscope. Sharmila remembered her Transformational Grammar professor from the university saying, "A sentence was not just a sentence. It had meaning, surface meaning, hidden meaning, and textual burials in ink."

Sharmila looked again at the sign. She could hear her professor chuckling his approval. Noam Chomsky, the brilliant linguist, the outspoken guru at MIT whom she admired so much, would analyze this to the point of oblivion. There was a seedy pub beside the store. A lot of construction workers and some deadbeats hung around there. One of them, seeing her look so closely at the sign, whistled and called out, "Can't you read English? Lady, I can help you read that English sign, you know!" She had merely smiled, pretended not to understand what he saying (like a new *desi)* and gone in. She did the same thing with telemarketers on the telephone. Didn't they know that she was like a sentence? That she had surface meaning, literal meaning and textual burials in flesh?

There were familiar smells inside the shop: Tibet soap and Tibet vanishing cream, half-burnt samosas, *chanachur*. She had picked up some fresh coriander leaves and some green chillies. A few of the vegetables, like the half-dried pumpkin and the coveted *Potol* were shrivelled up in a corner.

The dish that her husband had demanded would not be possible. The vegetables were not fresh enough. Sharmila hoped nervously that her husband could not mind. So it would be simple Bengali fare. *Dal*, rice, *bhaji*, fried fish and, of course, chicken, the constant without which the meat-eating fiends would howl. "Fish, fish, again fish—O Mummy, I want Bangla curry chicken." How warming, on *kulfi*-cold nights, was Bangla food prepared from scratch. None of those fancy French names, just plain semi-vowels and Bengali fricative consonants thrown in to make it sound pleasurable. She uttered the sounds of the palate:

"E...leee sh Bhaaaajii...

"Koo...ro...la...Bhaa...jii...

"Eeeees...h!"

Hot steam was escaping from the frothing basmati rice on the electric stove. It was almost done. Twenty-six minutes for two cups of rice and five cups of water. Sharmila still cooked rice the *Dadi-Nani* way, the traditional way her grandmothers did, by letting the rice boil in the water and then draining the starchy water away. Nothing was added; the rice retained its *desi* sanctity. If rice was eaten regularly, this was the best way to cook it. One would never get heavy or fat.

The steam now began to form patterns above the sink. She read the lines of her life in the steam as easily as a fortune teller reads tea leaves. The change in her husband had come slowly like the acrid smell of gas seeping from an ancient oven. Even the comfortable husband smell had changed into a scent that she could no longer define.

At first it had been the despair of never finding a job. Her body had borne the frustrated traces of the paths that he had forged through the city on his job-finding expeditions. And then the miracle! A corporate job! But then his eyes changed. At a corporate party that they had attended together, he kept away from her, as if he was almost ashamed of her. He laughed easily with the bleached corporate cougars whose nips and tucks squeaked at every laugh. He looked at her but once, with a certain annoyance at her *desi* sari.

Pain seeped in as it always did, little by little, in droplets. Fluid, nascent, pungent. It gripped her by the throat and scraped away her throat cells. Hurting, she wanted to grip a knife and slit away her pain. Pain also swept in the smell of the homeless woman and fear jabbed her throat. How was she to keep it all together? Her other self? Her family? This new city?

Sharmila washed her warm face at the kitchen sink. She could hear the wind-snow flying at the windowpanes. She hoped that he would not notice her swollen, puffy eyes at the dinner table. Her hands shook a little. Sharmila knew how much he hated puffy eyes. The molecules of steam had now dissipated into domestic ether space.

The rice was done.

• • •

NOTES ON THE TEXT

Desi—Widely used term for people and things such as food, movies and culture associated with South East Asia (India, Bangladesh, Pakistan, Sri Lanka). The *Toronto Star* reported one million people in the Greater Toronto Area fall under this category.

Sambar masala—Spices associated with South Indian and Sri Lankan cooking.

Angreezi—A colonial term meaning the English. Here it refers to all white people.

Bollywood—The Indian movie industry.

Bangladesh—Former East Bengal (United India). When the British left India in 1947, United India was divided to become India and Pakistan. East Bengal was a Muslim majority area and became part of Pakistan. After the War of Liberation in 1971, East Pakistan became Bangladesh.

Nani—Maternal grandmother (original Sanskrit, used widely in Bengali, Urdu, Hindi and Punjabi).

Sona—Term of endearment (Bengali, Punjabi, Urdu and Hindi).

Amar kache gumao—Lie down beside me (Bengali)

Sufi Shahjalal—(1271–1347). He was an important Sufi saint of Bengal. He was born as Sheikh Makhdum Jalaluddin in Yemen and travelled with dervishes from Turkey to Bengal to spread Islam. He lies buried at Sylhet, Bangladesh.

Nakshikatha—Decorative embroidery done with small stitches.

Asho Amar ghore asho—Welcome to my home (Bengali). Lines from a well-known song by Rabindranath Tagore.

Kushu na—Nothing.

Hurs—Heavenly pure companions (source: the Qu'ran).

Porees—Fairies (source: Bengali fairy tales).

Kota, Tangail, Rajshahi silk, Mirpur Kathan, Jamdani—Saris from Bangladesh.

Indo-Aryan—Around the year 2000 BC, a sun-worshipping Indo-European tribe calling themselves Aryans, using a language known as Sanskrit, invaded central Asia and occupied territory as far as the north of India. The Indo-Aryans were the descendants of these tribes. The term is used linguistically to refer to a wide collection of people united by their common status as speakers of the Indo-Aryan branch of the family of Indo-European languages. Today there are more than 1.4 billion native speakers of Indo-Aryan languages (Bengali, Urdu, Hindi, etc.). Many of them are native to South East Asia, where they form a majority.

Tagore—Rabindranath Tagore (1861–1941), Bengali Nobel Prize laureate for literature in 1913. The national anthem of India and Bangladesh were composed by him.

Nazrul—Kazi Nazrul Islam (1899–1976). Popularly known as the Bengali rebel poet, who espoused rebellion against religious orthodox traditions and the British Raj in India.

Rosogollah—Bengali sweets.

Potoler dolma—Vegetable dish.

Chanachur—Spicy snack.

Dal—Soup made with pulses.

Bhaji—Vegetable dish.

Kulfi—Indian ice cream.

Dadi—Paternal grandmother.

Zoe's Dance

Elpida Morfetas

Zoe had learned long ago that it was unwise to voice her thoughts about weddings. After all, who would listen to a woman who never dreamed of being the bride? As a girl, she often played wedding with the neighbourhood children. The others always fought for the same roles—bride, parents of the bride, flower girl or organist. Zoe only ever wanted to be the priest. She'd put on her grandmother's oversized black wool cardigan and demand an answer to the words she'd seen on television soaps: *Do you take this man?* The impatient guests wiped away sweat in the late afternoon summer heat. The groom, who'd been promised his fair share of chips and gum, tried not to look bored. Now, at thirty, Zoe waited for the weddings around her to pass. Once all her cousins were married, she thought, life might assume some quiet and stability.

She checked herself for the last time in the hallway mirror before leaving her house. Wiping away some of the inky liner around her eyes, she tried not to look down at her bright blue sleeveless dress. It betrayed its past by being too tight, and she often found herself having to pull it down and shift it into place. Still, she liked the way it held her in its grip. Its pattern of large dark indigo flowers exploded around her torso and hips. Wearing the dress reminded her of the summer she spent in Italy with a married lover she'd known would never marry her.

At her car, she cleared away all the loose papers and brushed off most of the dog hair, so her half-sister and cousin could sit comfortably on the front and back seats. She was driver for the third FWO of the summer. The last Family Wedding of Obligation. It was a bright Saturday in mid June. The date was just as ordinary as the wedding plans. There had already been the prenuptial send-off at the paternal home, as well as the church ceremony, where the couple remained silent while the priest murmured in heavily accented English and Byzantine Greek. All that remained was the banquet hall meal and dance.

On the way to pick up her sister, she thought about the happy bride, her cousin Lianna. The groom—always a secondary player at these events—was an internet match. Lianna and her man had read each other's profiles on D.I.Y. Love-Match, which invited clients to "become your own matchmaker" for a small fee. D.I.Y. had separate sections for matches by race, ethnicity and religion. The two met in the Greek section and sent each other a list of what they wanted in a partner and what they hoped for out of life. He wrote that he chose the site because meeting his own kind meant there would be fewer crazies. This didn't really make Lianna want to LOL, but she told him it did. They arranged a face-to-face meeting to double-check compatibility. Lianna wore her long black hair loose and straight because she'd read in his profile that he liked women with long hair. He reminded Lianna of everything her father was: short, bald, restrained, kindly toward those he liked, indifferent toward all others. And after Zoe met his mother at the bridal shower—a petite woman who wore a frozen grin and a bright pink wool suit—she realized her cousin was everything the older woman was not: intelligent, opinionated, organized and pear shaped.

After joking about online love matches on the phone one night, Lianna confided to Zoe that she had been meeting this man for months, testing the shark-infested waters of compatibility. But secret meetings were difficult to accomplish, even in a city the size of Toronto. Within a few weeks friends had seen the couple walking and talking, holding hands. Lianna would release his hand when she thought she spotted someone she knew in the distance; he'd take a deep breath, as though preparing for a fall, and give an anguished smile. Zoe knew her cousin was uncertain about being seen with him in public.

The wedding was arranged within a year, as Lianna was determined to be married before she turned thirty. Her family and friends warned her that it might be too soon to marry her virtual stranger—someone she hadn't met at school or work or through a friend—but Lianna steadied herself with the catchphrase she'd used in her D.I.Y. Love-Match profile: "When you know, you know."

Zoe remembered the look on her mother's face when she'd torn open the lily-white invitation.

"I don't understand this internet finding business," Zoe's mother sneered. "How did Lianna pay the matchmaker?" Zoe made no attempt to explain.

Weddings in the city happened all year. Like funerals, attending them was almost inevitable. That's how Zoe talked herself into going to the first, the next and the one after that. But they always seemed to cause friction. The women in her family would fight it out: what to wear (and what not to), when to skip the church service, when to arrive at the hall, when to leave, how much money to give. Her mind raced over the worst-case-scenarios of the day.

She tried to make the best of things when she picked up her sister.

"At least it's not one of those out-of-town weddings." She smiled brightly as Minerva settled into the passenger side.

"Shit, yeah, those take up a whole weekend. So, sis, you ready? Got your still-single-and-barren face on? I see you're wearing the dress."

"I didn't have time to get a new one."

"Yeah, sure."

When they picked up Fofo, Minerva slid obligingly into the backseat to let her cousin ride shot-gun rather than hear her complaints about becoming car sick.

Fofo strapped herself into the front seat, turned and looked Minerva over from head to foot. "Nice suit."

"Thanks. So, Zo was just saying that at least this will be a short ride."

"Yes, it's an in-town wedding for Lianna. At least we don't have to drive to Prince Edward County, or London, or Stratford," Zoe mused.

"Anglo weddings," Fofo said, tagging these locations with the sense of finality she used to classify the insurance claims at work. "Greek weddings almost always happen in the city, especially when like marries like."

"You mean when predictable marries unimaginative," Minerva said in a mocking tone.

"What?" Fofo said pretending not to hear. She nervously fiddled with the clasp of her tiny antique silver purse. "Tradition is still important to some of us, you know. Anyway, cuz, you're not ruining the day for me."

Fofo's instinct was to feign indifference to criticism, a trait she inherited from her grandmother, along with large breasts, a heart-shaped birthmark on her lower back and thick red hair. Fofo never met the woman who'd used every natural gift she had to survive two wars in Greece. Fofo's mother carried her genetic legacy to Toronto. She came through customs after a ten-hour flight from Athens, speaking no English other than "thank you, mister," to a country where she knew no one but her husband. The woman found a way to survive. It was evident in the way she squinted her eyes and used her strong, sharp chin to point out the olives she wanted to the local grocer before she learned English.

"Whatever. I'm wasting my time. None of these people are ever going to come to my wedding," Minerva continued.

"Oh come on, Min. I'd come to your wedding. I *love* gay weddings!" Fofo cooed.

Zoe tried not to look in the rearview mirror, hoping to shield herself from Minerva's petrifying gaze. She fixed her eyes on the road ahead.

Minerva sat up straight. "I'm talking about the big deal people make about these events. At the hall, they shove big fat envelopes with hundreds of dollars into a box. Might as well sign the card with, *Good for you, honey. You finally found someone boring enough to want the same things you do: a car, a house, a nine-to-five job.* Then they produce drooling, spoiled little monsters with the grandparents looking after them just like in the old country, while the parents work so they can buy more stuff."

"Talk about negative," Fofo began.

"Hey," Zoe broke in, "why didn't you ask Adrienne to come with us today, Min?"

"So she could sit at the loser table with the unwed?" Minerva leaned her head back and ran her fingers through her short curly hair. "She wanted to come but I told her not to bother. What's the point?" Her voice trailed off as she looked out the window.

As sisters, they'd had this conversation many times before. Bringing Adrienne would have meant fighting the urge to touch her, to hold her hand, kiss her, dance with her and fake-flirt with other women. Zoe never pressured Minerva, the way their mother did; she knew her sister's gut feeling was to avoid most family functions.

"This is the wedding of your first cousin. No excuses this time—not one word!" their mother had said.

"Well, what I love is the dancing. Eh, Zoe will you dance this time, or are you just going to sit and watch as usual? You know, I have never danced even one *sirtaki* with you. What are you going to do? Sit out your own wedding when that day comes? Don't get stuck in the past, girl. People can only mourn for..."

"Shut up, Fofo! Leave her alone." Minerva kicked Fofo's seat.

"Stop it, both of you!" They stopped at another light. Zoe breathed deeply. She looked back at Minerva and smiled.

There was silence for the next twenty-minute stretch of road. They passed a Ukrainian church, a mosque and then a small strip mall. They arrived at the Isis Banquet Hall on Danforth Road, the place where Zoe's family held all their functions.

The Isis was owned by a tiny Greek-Egyptian man. Mr. Tolis was always ready to greet everyone with a loud *Hallo!* Whenever he smiled, and he often did, he inadvertently frightened small children with his two large gold incisors. The giant billboard outside his banquet hall read *Isis Banquet Hall* and below this, in smaller print, *Come and celebrate every occasion with the Mistress of Magic.* Isis, Egyptian goddess and sister-wife to the Lord of the Dead, was pictured in hieroglyphic style. Seated on her throne, she held a royal staff in one hand and a black ankh in the other. Her large, almond-shaped eyes, carefully outlined in kohl, surveyed the arrivals before they entered the hall.

After the meal there were speeches. Then the intermittent *clink clink* of glasses and plates to draw attention back to the bride and groom. The guests rose to dance the same slow and steady twelve-step circle dances their grandparents had danced at their weddings. A man with a guttural voice sang *Beautiful is our bride and beautiful is her dowry...let them both live in happiness.* Toward the end of the dance, the dancers picked up the pace, holding hands in a series of imperfect circles, dragging along some of the non-Greek guests. The glass chandeliers glistened and shook as the wooden floor vibrated to the rhythm of songs about dowries, grassy meadows, a quilt made for two and a beautiful, happy bride.

The DJ played only one transition song before moving to the heavier and slower rhythms of the *rembetika*. The men took command of the floor with the steady, determined steps of the solitary dance, the *zeimbekiko*. Occasionally they spun around after a quick three steps forward, three steps back. Zoe knew she had to watch—turning one's back on a dancer was like breaking a sacred trust.

Now the men moved to music from another time and a place even further away. These were the sounds of Turkish hashish dens, songs inspired by the lives of pimps and petty thieves.

The *zeimbekiko* defied the careful measured steps of other dances. No one would teach it to Zoe, not that she'd ever summoned the courage to ask. She had resisted this dance all her life. Once her uncle said to her, "You don't have to know any steps. Like life, there are no steps you can follow. Go back to what this life has cost you, and all that's been lost by those before you. Hold your arms up, like an eagle uses its wings to float on the wind, and move."

Watching the defiant, solitary dancers move, Zoe remembered the last time she had seen her father dance. She was four, her father was thirty, and they were about to leave their homeland. He had loved this one, the dance of refugees. At his sister's wedding—his last night in the village—he embraced each of his relatives warmly. The whiskey he had been drinking made him unusually affectionate and talkative. When he fell to his knees, gasping, the groom ran over to him, while the singer gestured for the musicians to stop.

Zoe saw Lianna's father tear her father's stiff white shirt. Pounding with both his hands on her father's motionless chest, he called out his brother-in-law's name. Her father's body convulsed and his face turned a faded violet. Her aunt Eleni held his head and cried, her wedding veil falling across her brother's face, shielding him from his family and the other guests as he died. The villagers said joy mingled with sorrow and stopped his heart in the middle of the dance. When Eleni and her husband left for Canada, Zoe's mother left too. With her daughter, she put the ocean and a new Canadian man between her and these memories. Three years later, Minerva was born with the hope of helping them embrace the future and their new home.

Minerva stood up to dance, moving like a dove moving through a flock of ravens. The men, wearing their grey or black suits, stepped briskly to the verge of the dance floor. They continued to dance, but glanced sideways at the tall slender woman in the white wool. She spun around them with her eyes closed and her arms raised. She had removed her jacket. Her dark skin glistened and her thick silver hoop earrings caught flashes of light. She leaned forward and took heavy, determined steps forward and back, snapping her fingers to the rhythm. Then she spun.

Zoe watched as her sister danced. She saw how Minerva didn't care who was watching; she didn't hear the ladies' whispering or see the men who scowled. She was an outsider who danced defiantly.

"Your sister, she dances like a man, eh, Zoeoula?" Fofo's mom was standing behind Zoe's chair. "She's good, this one." She gestured in Minerva's direction with her chin. Then she put her hands on Zoe's shoulders. "Come on now, you dance too."

Zoe smiled at her aunt, stood up and walked toward the banquet hall doors. Minerva's dance ended. The DJ began playing the snaking rhythms of the *tsifteteli*, the belly dance. Women of all ages crowded the dance floor.

Zoe walked past the smokers who were entertaining one another with jokes and stories outside. She walked along the curved, empty driveway, where a stream of never-ending limousines had delivered countless brides and grooms. Breathing the night air, she looked up at the stars; a few tiny punctures of bright light disturbed the perfect blackness of the sky. Isis's steady gaze was on her. She heard the music, felt its pulsating echo. She began to dance.

On a Day in May
Encounters
Loreli C. Buenaventura

ON A DAY IN MAY

My friend, my friend, I cannot stop the rain. I cannot catch your grey clouds in the cup of my palm and prevent the murky drops from seeping through the ridges of my hand. I cannot turn back time to foreshadow what has happened. Nor can we close our eyes to still the frames in our lives. I can only place my olive-skinned hand upon your cheek and tell you I understand.

And that is the problem, we understand too well. We can't explain it away because we know what it's about. And as much as we know why such events happen, there's only so much within our control. Events have a way of unfolding, as they often do. We'd like to think they can be indiscriminate, but you and I know that this isn't always true.

That Sunday, I waited for you. How I waited in anticipation. After a year separated by distance, I relished every moment to be spent with you. One o'clock, two o'clock, where are you? Three o'clock, four o'clock...and then as if on cue, I hear from you by phone, your voice muffled by the sound of cars speeding by. Though your words are inaudible amidst the clamour and bustle, I know that something has gone awry from the heaviness in your sigh.

What? At the corner of St. George and Bloor, in front of the shoe museum, you say. On your bicycle, then stopped by two police officers, you continue. This doesn't make sense, I interrupt. Were you wearing your helmet?

Past the murmur of conversations, I make out the words that spell your tale. A dark man, they say, was seen lifting a Swarovski crystal from an upscale Yorkville boutique and you on your bicycle seemed to fit the description. But what description was that? A dark man and only that?

And so the story goes...Your six foot frame in your baggy jeans and airy white cotton shirt, riding crouched on your bicycle; your dreads flying in the wind, your dark brown skin glowing upon contact with the sun's hot rays. Then, you were suddenly stopped by two police officers.

This must be some mistake, you explain. You were nowhere near neighbouring Yorkville but on your way to a friend's place this bright day. As your story goes on and on, I now understand where you had gone.

There's an intensity and firmness in your normally soft, hushed words. With every rise in the octave of your voice, shudders pass through my body. I am scared. I am weary. I can no longer take your story.

Detained for an hour, the police recounting every detail. They ask question after question, confident that you're guilty. And so at the corner of St. George and Bloor, steps away from the shoe museum, on one of the sunniest days of May, they search your knapsack, checking every item while throngs of passersby gather to pass their judgement. Only when they see that you're a member of faculty at a university do they question their take on your story. But still they continue, emptying all contents from your bag. Not until they peruse your book collection—Carol Shields, Kristeva, Freud—do they believe your words to be true.

We know such instances can happen; we know all the reasons and explanations. Such moments should be shrugged off our shoulders. But instead, you are still trembling from humiliation and I am still shaken by your story. Shaken, because my notion of home has just been transgressed—even on one of the most beautiful, most anticipated, sunny days of May.

My friend, my friend, I cannot stop the rain. I can only place my olive-skinned hand upon your cheek and tell you I understand. We can hold each other until the trembling stops and the last of the thick, salty tears fall from the lashes beneath your eyes.

ENCOUNTERS

It's that feeling. Your hands sweat, your heart pounds. You feel as though you're floating in two places at once but not belonging to one or the other... I want you, I need you, I care for you—but I shouldn't be here.

As you lie next to me, sound asleep, I am mesmerized by the steady rhythmic sound of your breathing. I watch the rise and fall of your chest, the candle's light flickering faintly on your face. You look so rested and peaceful, nothing like the anxiety consuming me. I try to relax and match the tempo of your breathing. But I am feeling constricted, at times gasping for air. The tightness in my throat tells me to leave. Instead, I slowly lift my hand, my fingertips tracing the contours of your warm, naked body.

Even in partial darkness, I am aware of the difference in the colour of our skin. As my fingertips slide from your hips to your thighs, I notice how much darker my skin is from yours. I notice how your summer tan almost hides the hair on your legs. I notice wrinkles on your body in places where my skin remains taut. You stir suddenly and turn around. I stroke your wavy brown hair away from your face. You mumble, and then your arms are around me in a tight embrace. Inside, I can hear myself whispering softly, "No, please, I need to go."

I am motionless, wide awake, feeling imprisoned by your chest against my back. My eyes scan the room...the silk ties, the designer cuff links, the meticulously polished soft leather shoes. My eyes rest on the tailored suits overflowing from your half-open closet—each one a reminder of a world I do not share with you.

The mark of my magenta lipstick left on a long-stemmed wine glass glares at me from the corner of the room. I can still smell traces of the incense burning earlier. As always, you have worked hard to please me. "Why can't you just trust me?" you plead. It's not that simple, I try to explain to you. But you do not hear. Or maybe you choose not to listen?

It was not always like this. I remember your light touch and how your eyes met mine as we danced to the murmur of our words. Or the times when we ignored the world around us and we revealed ourselves to each other in stark honesty and raw vulnerability. In our nakedness, I felt embraced and at times swallowed by love. Later I discovered such happiness could only be sustained by silencing a part of myself, not being fully present.

When it all started to unravel? Little by little? Our evenings together soon left me trembling and I wanted to flee. At times I also wanted to stay. I wished I could remain in your arms and in your refuge forever. But this safety revealed itself to be illusory. How much longer could I ignore words that erased my experiences? How often was I left staring at the phone after conversations in which you could not hear the pain in my words? I know you truly tried to understand. I know you wanted to connect. I, too, wanted to close that distance.

For all the times I felt alone to put the pieces back together and for all the times I could no longer be myself with you, I now prepare my exit from your life. Is it really about the difference in the colour of our skin? Or our attempt to deny that such differences exist and can colour the distance in our experiences?

As these thoughts run through my mind, I know I am angry, I know I am sad. And yet I am also relieved. I am weary of how the world has placed us in this corner and I yearn to be free. How is it I can hate you and yet love you at the same time? How can I want to stay but know I have to leave? Was my time with you about my own search for who I am? By being with you, I, too, for a fleeting moment could feel I belong. And how I so wanted to belong.

As the candle sends out its last flicker, tears and longing overwhelm me. I am immersed in total darkness. In closing my eyes, I try to capture in my mind the feeling of your body against mine. I listen as you breathe softly as if in a state of calm. I am tempted to caress you so that I could feel my lips against yours one last time. But instead, I dress abruptly and close the door to your room behind me.

Pain Management

Michael Redhill

Dennis Hanley had used up three of his four weeks at the institute, a small salmon-coloured building on University Avenue's hospital row. His Worker's Comp had paid for the first two weeks, and his parents were paying for the other two. At the institute they didn't call group therapy "Group" they called it "Conference," and everyone was supposed to dress in regular day-clothes—there were no robes or gowns to be had at all—although by the third week some people just kept their pajamas on all day.

Dr. Krayman was a young man with a easy-going manner and a huge black mustache. In Conference he said, "Pain is a signal, and a signal is a message that has to be decoded. So let's some of us describe some of the signals we're getting from our bodies."

A guy named Ernst spoke first. "I get a signal from my body that says I'm carrying a heavy weight."

"All right," said Dr. Krayman. "And how is that manifested in your body, Ernst."

"I have pain in my back and legs that won't go away." Ernst nodded like this was something shameful.

"Maybe if you knew what that weight was, you could throw it off."

"I sure would like to."

Dr. Krayman sent him a warm smile. The smile said *breakthrough*, but Ernst had already had this breakthrough; he just kept coming back to it like a dog sniffing its own scent on a lamppost. Krayman looked around the room. It was an unfortunate room. It was hard to know how many of the people in it were actually hearing Krayman; many of them looked overwhelmed by signals more intense than his voice. "We haven't heard from Melanie in a few days."

Melanie was sitting directly across from Dennis. Her hair had bright blue highlights. "My head hurts," she said, shrugging.

"Okay," said Krayman. "You're describing *pain*. But what is it trying to tell you?"

"That I should rip the fucking thing off."

"Everyone, Melanie is giving us a *signal*. And the signal is that she's *angry* about the pain she feels in her head. We can read her body language, the tone of her voice, and we understand completely what she's feeling. But we can't read her pain, because Melanie is not *decoding* the pain. And it is *her* pain, so we can't do this for her." He turned back to her. Dennis figured, like everyone else here, that Melanie was just dying of something that science hadn't named yet and the institute had figured out a way to charge everyone money until it did. "I thought it was interesting that you called your head a 'thing,'" he said.

"It *is* a thing. It's a thing that doesn't work."

"And yet it's a part of you."

Melanie cast a murderous look around the room. There was something in the tone of Dr. Krayman's questions that suggested if you only tried harder, you'd be rid of your debilitating problem, whatever it was. It cost two thousand Canadian dollars a week to stay here, and Dennis believed the institute knew that the kind of person crazy enough to pay that kind of money was the kind of person who'd already lost hope.

Dr. Krayman was waiting patiently for Melanie to volunteer something else, but she was looking down now, hoping that her turn on the hot seat was over. Finally, the doctor said, "All of you are here because your pain won't respond to conventional medicine. In fact, conventional medicine says there's nothing wrong with you. It won't even venture a guess as to whether your pain is *real*. Now isn't that interesting. You have a feeling, and science doubts it. Science is in denial." He looked around the room, and then he suddenly raised a finger. "But, ah," he said now, "maybe so are *you*."

"I'm not in denial," Melanie muttered.

"Then say it," said Dr. Krayman. "What do we say in here?"

Melanie raised her head and they all saw tears rolling down her cheeks. She seemed to cry in here every day, even when she didn't speak. She said, "I have pain, but the pain isn't me."

Dennis's pain was a continuous burning in all of his extremities, including his nose and his penis. The obvious diagnosis had been MS, but you weren't supposed to get MS in your nose or your dick, and after months and months of tests, the doctors told him what he had was chronic undifferentiated pain and they prescribed antidepressants. Still he burned, as if the various edges of his being were held endlessly to lit matches.

Hot baths helped, and Dennis took them three times a day. In a hot bath, the temperature of the rest of his body was brought up to the level of his misheated parts, and it made him feel temporarily normal again.

His girlfriend, Theresa, often sat on the rim of the tub and massaged Dennis's shoulders. There was a time when she'd sit on the edge behind him with her pant legs rolled up and her feet in the tub, but now she found the water too hot. She remembered the movie about Terry Fox and how, near the end, he couldn't get water hot enough to lessen his pain, and she wondered if maybe Dennis was dying. It was possible that, at some late, unpredictable moment, his symptoms would coalesce into something lethal and he'd die on her in some spectacular fashion. She'd even had a dream of him bursting into flames at the kitchen table. In the dream, she'd pushed her chair back in stunned horror and stood up, but he'd just looked down at himself and said, "Oh, shit," and collapsed into a little pyramid of ash.

"I read that some phantom pain is caused by grinding your teeth when you sleep," she said to him one afternoon in the institute. His parents had paid for a semiprivate room, so he had only a single roommate, while some of the patients (*oops*, Dennis would catch himself thinking, *clients*) had to sleep in a dorm room for four or six. A crinkly blue curtain could be drawn around the bed for some privacy.

"That's migraines," Dennis said. He was resting, and he hoped that Theresa would come back tomorrow so he could sleep a while before they rang the buzzer for dinner. The regimen at the institute was exhausting, and they kept track of everything, including your bodily functions. Nothing was beyond suspicion. "They have bite plates you can wear when you sleep so your back teeth don't touch. And my pain isn't 'phantom.' I really feel it."

"I know you do, Denny," she said. "I didn't mean it that way."

He closed his eyes to show he was ready for a nap, but he could sense she wasn't ready to go yet.

"Do you think you're making progress?" she asked.

"I think I'm learning a lot."

"Like what?"

"Well..." He opened his eyes. She'd crossed her legs in the chair beside the bed and folded her hands over her knees. This was a long conversation posture; he knew it well. "In Conference I'm learning to think of the pain as a relationship I'm in, a toxic relationship. And I have to figure out how to break it off."

"And are you figuring it out?"

"I'm not sure yet."

"Because you only have six more days you know." He nodded, waiting for her to make her point. "Eight thousand dollars is a lot of money."

He breathed out through his nostrils and felt the heated air ricochet off the pillow and into his left eye. He'd guessed long ago that Theresa didn't really think he had pain. She thought he had a *problem,* and she was interested in knowing what it was, but he wasn't sure how to put it in terms that would have satisfied her. In some ways, he saw it from her point of view and sympathized. How'd he like to have a mysteriously malingering girlfriend? Anyone would get frustrated with it. "I *am* feeling better. Not a hundred percent, but better. Hell, even the rest helps."

"You look better."

"Do I?" he said on an upnote.

"A little." She pushed down on her knees, which levered her upright. The sight of her tall body rising beside his bed sent a little thrill through him, which translated itself into a sensation of heat in his fingers. Theresa leaned down and kissed him tenderly on his lips. She looked concerned. "All I want is for you to feel like yourself again."

"That day is coming," he said.

The last time they'd made love, the week before he moved to the institute, Dennis had held his jaw tightly shut the whole time, kissing Theresa with hard lips. "We can stop," she'd said, but he shook his head no. He stroked her body with his fingertips, enduring the pain even the faintest friction caused him. He expected to see that pain translated onto her skin in little licks of flame, as if his fingers were match heads. And yet he'd not even broken a sweat. Theresa's skin glistened beneath him, he saw the prickling flush of red flesh across her chest—proof of her arousal, rather than his being incendiary—and then she gave him her signal, a squeeze of his upper arm, that said he could stop.

He'd actually begged her to let him start using condoms again, but condoms weren't much better, offering only faint protection from her, and the added resistance of the material created more troubles. She'd patiently seen him from doctor to doctor, holding hands with him in various waiting rooms (and then stopping when he told her it hurt) until finally she seemed to accept that something unusual was happening. He gave notice at his work (he was a garden-variety IT specialist) and when the institute recommended a month-long stay, he asked his parents to pay the difference.

His first few days on the floor were distinguished by an unending parade of stories odder than his own. Melanie had headaches that tested "worse than migraines" according to the results of a self-administered multiple-choice quiz that she kept in a pocket. She took it out from time to time, for confirmation, it seemed. Dennis's roommate, Geoffrey, had chronic pain in his tongue that made it difficult for him to eat. But Geoffrey's tongue always looked normal to Dennis, who'd watch him tenderly brushing his teeth in the mirror and noting the tongue's shape and colour. Small, smooth, pink.

His roommate might've been playing the system, Dennis sometimes thought. He knew Geoffrey was there on a Worker's Comp release, and he'd gotten four weeks out of them, which was unusual. Somewhere along the way, Geoffrey had convinced a tribunal of three people that a painful tongue made it impossible to work. Dennis tried to imagine what kind of pain that would have to be. Surely something that made it impossible to talk, but he noted that Geoffrey had no trouble speaking. On their third night in the semiprivate room, Geoffrey had said, "With or against your will?" and Dennis hadn't understood what he meant. "Did you want to come, or did they make you come?"

"Oh," he said. "Maybe a little of both. Comp gave me two weeks, but my parents insisted on four. I already know none of this is going to help."

Geoffrey made a clucking noise with his mouth and then laughed. "You come out of here with pain, they can probably have you committed. Rubber clamp in the mouth and everything."

"They'd have to make an exception in your case," Dennis said.

"I can take anything now."

"I bet."

He sort of liked Geoffrey, or at least found something to like while he was tolerating him for twenty-eight days. Sometimes his roommate seemed slick and other times he just seemed dumb, but dumb like a fox, as his mother would have said.

"Whaddayou think of Melanie?" Geoffrey asked on another night. This through two layers of curtains.

"She's fine."

"You like her, don't you?"

"I have a girlfriend, Geoff."

"Come on, you like her."

Dennis couldn't help himself: he laughed nervously. "Okay, I like her. But she's all yours. I presume that's why you're asking."

There was silence from the other side of the room for a long time, just a low breathing. A couple of times, Dennis even thought the breathing was getting closer. "You asleep?" he finally asked.

"No, no, just thinking. You're right, you know, about Melanie. That's why I asked."

People with pain, as a rule, had a hard time waking up. In Conference it was floated that since pain was something most people were only aware of when they were awake, then perhaps pain was something constructed by the waking mind. And painkillers—those semi-anesthetics—worked only because they induced a partial dream state and allowed the waking mind to let go of a little of its anguish.

All this made Dennis wonder. Could he be as sick as these other people? Half of them were crazy; this much was clear. But his pain was real, waking or not, he was sure of that; maybe the institute's job was to separate the loons from the medical rarities, and then send that tiny remainder back into the gears of the caring professions. In the hands of doctors, Dennis had submitted himself to the entire gamut of pain-prognostication. Behind a flower-vined red-brick wall on a side street near Yonge and Eglinton, he'd been pricked viciously by an old Jewish doctor with body maps on the wall. The man told him there was nothing wrong with him. And inside a pale blue room in a teaching hospital at the University of Toronto, a class of students in gowns that were too large for them watched eagerly as their professor scraped, pinched, heated, thumped and punctured various parts of him while he was connected to a machine. The theme of the examination became the problem of "normal": "Normally, this would cause electrical activity in the patient's brain to spike a little" and "although this is clearly painful, the temperature of the patient's skin at the contact point remains constant, contrary to normal expectations."

One of the students—a young man who might have been twelve—asked, "Would we expect to see retarded dendrite growth in the subject?"

And another: "Do you think this is going to eventually kill him?"

The more he failed to register on various Geiger counters and litmus papers as well as to respond to experimental treatments, and the more Dennis despaired of being cured, the more interesting he became to doctors. Some appeared to be thrilled to have their treatments come up empty. He was on the verge of being someone's discovery.

He collected the requisite three doctor's letters and submitted his claim
to Worker's Comp. They called him two days later to tell him to report to
the institute whenever he was ready. His daily schedule there was a regimen
of physiotherapy, aquatherapy (his thrice-daily baths), individual and
group therapy, nutritional counselling, acupressure and homeopathic blood
therapy. This made for a full day, and some of the clients of the institute
found their minds taken off the pain long enough that it seemed the cure
was simply distraction. But others were more tenacious cases. Like Melanie
and Geoffrey. Their pain had been labelled "resistant" by the institute, and
when the institute got ready to admit defeat, you had to know there was
something uniquely wrong with you.

Geoffrey and Melanie finally were gravitating toward each other. Dennis
would come back from aquatherapy and find Geoffrey talking quietly on the
bed, Melanie sitting sideways, prim almost. In the second and third weeks,
the institute experimented with an ice-filled collar for Geoffrey, thinking if
they dulled nerve impulses in the back of his neck, it might reduce the pain
in his tongue. It was a long, thin, balloon-like apparatus that came around
from behind and got tied under his chin. Its two blue ends tapered down to
points on either side of the front of his neck. It made him look like an insane
Frenchman wearing a frozen cravat.

Melanie abandoned the primness quickly (the blue hair tips were a hint to
Dennis that she wasn't that withdrawn) and most afternoons and evenings,
the curtain would be drawn around Geoffrey's bed. Dennis could hear them
in there, sometimes suspiciously quiet, other times talking so he could
hear. They never talked about him, but sometimes they'd be silent a while
and then one of them would laugh and he'd figure that meant they'd found
something about him to amuse themselves with. He wondered how it
was to them to kiss, Geoffrey with his sensitive tongue, her with the ever-
present headaches that caused her to hold her head at odd angles just to
channel the pain.

From the evidence, sex was as therapeutic as weeping for Melanie, and
during the last half of Dennis's stay, her fervent entreaties to Geoffrey to be
brought to orgasm in the next bed over became more and more urgent. It
wasn't sex as Dennis had ever understood it; it was closer to CPR. She wanted
to have her life saved. When they finished, the two of them would lie there
in near silence, Melanie quietly thanking Geoffrey for his efforts on her
behalf and Geoffrey murmuring that he loved her. Dennis supposed it would
have to be love. The almost complete lack of privacy meant that there was
no point in trying to be discreet.

"I can go for a walk," he'd say to them.

"You don't have to, honest. You're cool with this, right?"

"It's natural," Dennis said.

"If you want, have Theresa over, and you know, we can kind of drown each other out."

"Yeah, bring Theresa," Melanie said. "She's nice." Then a little silence and one of those laughs.

To say that he had lost all hope was not accurate, but it was the term of art bandied around in his final week, one loosed by frustrated therapists who had been trained to see resistant pain as a form of willfulness. Dennis's individual therapist had even asked him if he was sure he wanted to get better, and Dennis, flustered by the question, wondered if maybe the doctor had seen deeply into him and fished out a terrible truth. He *thought* he was certain he wanted to get better; he hated his pain. And yet the experts were not as certain as he was. Maybe it was possible that he belonged to that subset of people so in love with their pain, and so greedy for punishment (in repayment of *what* could take many years of analysis the therapist warned him) that Dennis might turn out to be a very special case indeed. When later he discovered that both Geoffrey and Melanie had been given the same diagnosis, he felt relieved: just another tactic of the institute that had to have results to underscore its fees.

Instead of feeling thwarted, however, he enjoyed the final week, treating it as a vacation (not that he used that word with Theresa). The acupressure sessions, although sometimes triggering little conflagrations in his fingers, were generally very pleasant, and a warm, even collegial, atmosphere had developed between him and the woman who worked on him. In his individual therapy sessions he gave some answers he knew would be viewed as progress as a kind of offering to the doctor, whose pen happily bobbed back and forth over her notepad. He was *giving back*, which was some of the generous lingo of the place. Pain was viewed sometimes as a form of taking, a form of keeping. Giving back was another way of letting go.

But sometimes, in the strict privacy of his own mind, Dennis wondered if it was sensible to try to let go. They kept saying that pain was a signal, a message, so why try to release it before you understood it? It seemed to him that the attempt to separate the pain from the sufferer might be a way of guaranteeing that the sufferer remained in the dark about something crucial. As the weeks went on and he witnessed some of the improvements in the others that had supposedly been wrought by the therapy, he thought those who were having their symptoms relieved all displayed a similar characteristic. He couldn't name it at first, but after a week of seeing a sort of furtive happiness on some of his fellow client's faces, he recognized it. It was the face you saw on television when they filmed a certain kind of person coming out of a courtroom—one who'd been let off on a technicality.

Even though airflow was strictly regulated on the floor, someone had gone around and opened the windows to let in the scent of spring. Dogwood and magnolia, life-affirming smells. His mother sat at an angle on the side of the bed, smoothing the light blue sheet absently with her fingertips. His dad stood by the window, which was on the other side of the room by Geoffrey's bed (which, for the entire visit, contained both Geoffrey and Melanie), and Theresa sat in the visitor's chair. "We can easily do another couple of weeks, hon," his mother was saying. "Dr. Frank thinks it's just a matter of time, and your dad and I..." She left the unsaid hanging. Money wasn't an issue.

"I'm ready to go though," he said.

"You could go right to the end of May, and then we'll put a tent up at the club and everyone can come and celebrate your re-entry into the painless world." She patted the mattress with her hand, a done deal, and turned to the other bed. Her face, to anyone who didn't know her, would have seemed bright with unquestioning faith in all good things. "You two as well," she said to Geoffrey and Melanie, "I expect to see you there!"

"It sounds so nice," said Melanie. "Thank you."

Dennis shifted his body away from his mother's. The way she was sitting had compressed the sheets around his middle. "I don't think we need a party," he said. "And I'm not staying past Friday. This is it for me."

"You're not better," said his father.

"I'm fine."

"I'm not paying for 'fine,' Dennis. I'm paying for 'better,' and you're not better. We've discussed this, your mum and I."

"I think he's better," Geoffrey said, and they all looked at him. "I mean, I don't think there's any such thing as a 'painless' world, Mrs. Hanley. But I've lived with Dennis a whole month, and I think he *is* better."

"Thank you, Geoff," said Dennis.

"Not perfect, but better."

"What do you think, Theresa?"

She hadn't seemed to be listening, but she turned to look at Geoffrey. Two more weeks in here, Dennis thought, catching the grey wattles under her eyes, and he'd be visiting her in some institution himself. "I need a party," she said. "I need to have about eight drinks and then dance until I feel like sleeping, and then I need to sleep for about two days."

Melanie nodded emphatically. "You said it."

That night, the curtains to both beds still open, the three of them lay in the dark talking. "Do you really think I'm better?"

"Not much," Geoffrey said. "We're the hopeless cases."

"At least we know what we are," Dennis said.

He lay there, drowsing. He let himself have a fantasy about his massage therapist, imagining her hand closing warmly around him and feeling nothing but the heat of her hand, the way it was supposed to be. He could hear Melanie and Geoffrey talking quietly, and after a few minutes they brought him out of his reverie, Melanie saying, "We're going to get out of here."

"Right now," said Geoffrey.

"Everything's done in two days," said Dennis. "And anyway, no one's holding you here. You can quit any time."

Melanie was already sitting up on the other side of the bed, pulling on ankle boots. "It's symbolic. We're going to escape from this place where we're supposedly here of our own free will. It's a gesture."

"A symbolic gesture," said Geoffrey. "Why don't you come with us?"

Dennis laughed. He imagined the look on his mother's face when she came in around dinner time tomorrow and they told her he'd left with his roommate and his roommate's girlfriend. "What the fuck," he said. "It's a nice night."

They waited for him to throw his stuff into his locker; they were going to travel light. They locked everything up and headed out into the darkened hallway to the elevators. On the main floor, the security guard looked at them over his magazine.

"We're escaping," said Melanie. "We're making a break for it."

"See yuh," said the uniformed man. He pressed a button to unlock the door to the outside.

Most of the downtown bus routes had all-night stops, one of the forward-looking municipal gestures from a few years back, when the city seemed to be thinking about what people needed. He waited with the two of them at a stop on College Street, glancing once in a while down the block to the other side to see if anyone was coming to get them. No one was.

It was the pale washed-out black of a Toronto night: no stars, just ambient light from everywhere making it look like the whole city was in a terrarium. After half an hour, the streetcar appeared down a curve and slowly made its way toward them. A few people sat alone inside, lit up like an exhibition, and the three of them got on and sat together. Melanie kept her eyes mostly closed. "She okay?" asked Dennis.

"Same," said Geoffrey.

Yonge Street slid by and the other passengers got off and a few more got on and if he'd closed his eyes through the stop and only reopened them when the car started moving again, it would have seemed to Dennis that nothing had changed onboard. Past one o'clock in the morning, entire categories of humanity were interchangeable within their subsets.

"We're going to this great speakeasy I know in the east end," said Geoffrey. "We all need a drink."

"Absolutely," said Melanie.

The east end was a part of town Dennis didn't know at all. But lots of people came from there and lived out there, and saying "east end" didn't mean anything in Toronto. If you kept going, you eventually got to a part of town that looked a lot like his childhood stomping grounds, with good little shops, old red-brick schools and expansive parks with kites tangled in tree branches. "Did you grow up out there?" he asked Geoffrey.

"We both did actually," he said. "Melanie and I have a lot in common, we discovered. But yeah, I've spent most of my life on Jones Avenue. Went to junior and high school out there."

"It's a big city. I don't even know where Jones is."

"You will shortly, young man."

"It's unforgettable," added Melanie and she laughed without opening her eyes.

He'd been keenly aware of how it must have sounded to them in the room earlier that day, his father prepared to toss another four thousand into the pit that was his undiagnosable condition. He thought he'd buy them all the drinks they wanted, and the three of them would get totally drunk and forget their woes. And then, with the sun rising, he'd make Geoff show them his favourite greasy spoon and Dennis would treat them to a grand slam breakfast. A little of everything for their suffering.

He watched the unfamiliar street names and neighbourhoods drift past in the window. Melanie was asleep now on Geoffrey's lap, and the couple of times Dennis looked over at him, Geoffrey smiled contentedly at him. Maybe all I need, he thought, is a wider world with more people in it. I just need context. My pain isn't special. For Chrissake, I live in North Toronto, I can play golf during the daytime, I have a great girlfriend. I'm one of the lucky ones.

They crossed the bridge over the Don River and then went through a Chinatown Dennis hadn't realized was out there. A city with two Chinatowns. After that, the streets started to look sparse and empty, and then the road angled into another neighbourhood full of Indian shops and restaurants. He saw the street sign for Jones go past. "That was your street," he said.

"Mm," said Geoffrey. "The place I'm thinking of is a little further on." They passed through a residential area and then a part of the street where rickety garages faced out onto the street instead of lawns. Geoffrey pulled the wire to signal the stop, then leaned down and kissed Melanie on the neck. She sat up, groggy, then looked back and forth to Geoffrey and Dennis. "Showtime," she said.

They walked in the direction they'd come from, passing some shack-like structures. Dennis thought he could hear music inside some of them. "Well-kept secrets, Dennis," said Geoffrey, nodding to a pink wooden structure. "These are tiny little clubs, some of them. Underground bars in all senses of the word."

Dennis felt admitted to something special, excited by the prospect of being somewhere he'd have no chance of getting to without this new con-nection. Geoffrey and Melanie held hands, trading a look now and again, and the three of them went down a little passageway that led behind a row of garages.

"What's this place we're going to called?" he said.

Geoffrey looked back over his shoulder at him. "They just have numbers." They came to a leather-covered door. It looked like a huge comfy chair with big buttons set into it. There was no number. "You're the guest of honour, roommate," Geoffrey said. "Go ahead and knock."

He'd once heard that being shot was much like being smashed with a wooden plank, the force of the bullet less a piercing than the application of a broad force. And what surprised him when he received the first blow was how little it hurt. In fact, before there was any pain at all, there was a smell, a puff of sulphur that went up into the middle of his head, and this was profoundly surprising, so surprising that his only utterance was *wow*. He'd raised his hand to knock on the wood beside the strange door, and the blow on the back of his head seemed to him a magical analogue of the gesture he was not to complete.

They gave him a royal beating. At first it seemed that Geoffrey was the more violent of the two, but Dennis was aware of him, if anything, holding back a little. His blows were more frequent, but they were often glancing, careening off Dennis's ear or crown. But Melanie was applying herself. He was surprised at how much energy she displayed, and he imagined it came at no small cost to her head. But it *was* her foot he felt driven into his lower back, which brought him finally to his knees, and then her two fists clenched into a heart-sized mallet that came down with such persuasion on the top of his head. She kicked him in the stomach and chest while Geoffrey muttered imprecations somewhere close by, offering only a half-hearted stomp to Dennis's pelvis, a disinterested kick to the spine.

All the while, Dennis experienced this from some place outside of himself. There was something clinical about it, something intellectual. He was naming his own body parts to himself as they drew the attention of his attackers, recalling the charts and exploded views he'd seen so much of in the last months. *That's the cervical vertebra, and a good one there to the fibula. That'd be the scapula.*

Now perhaps he'd die. And everyone would know exactly how it had happened. Nothing more would have to be taken on faith. They'd see the signs on his body—hieroglyphs on his body's Rosetta Stone—and the signs would tell a story.

The pain (which now finally came in like a wave, lapping first at his nerve endings and then crashing against them) was fantastic. He felt two of his ribs snap, and felt them snap as if he inhabited them and the breaking marrow split his own being in two. He was present within the muscles on the side of his upper leg *(Vastus lateralis!)* as a blow there crushed the base of the muscle where it tapered into the tendon that connected it to his femur. The tendon snapped and he experienced the sensation of that entire muscle retreating into his leg like a window shade shooting up.

In fact, the feeling of pain that accompanied the beating was so particular that he knew it was something he'd been missing for his whole life. He thought he might even thank his attackers, if he could speak; he wanted to wrap them in this sensation they were giving him, to show them what real feeling could be like.

And then, as if they were twin typhoons, Geoffrey and Melanie wore them-selves out and withdrew, stepping back a little to look at their handiwork.

"Rich fuck," said Geoffrey. Dennis looked through the slit of one eye at them. There was dirt in his eyelashes. Melanie had her arm around Geoffrey. There was blood on her shirt and her head was tilted forward at an odd angle. A headache, Dennis guessed. He tasted blood. There were things he wanted to say, but no way to say them. He bled on the oily dirt of the alley-way. His attackers came toward him and then went past him, back to the street, Dennis presumed. They hadn't even robbed him. His life had been like a cell that didn't have a receptor for experience.

His stay in the hospital was lengthy, but everything they did for him worked. His bones knit, his swelling went down. His mother, on one of her visits, brought him a letter from Theresa that explained she was moving on in her life. He claimed to have memory loss about the attack and never fingered Geoffrey or Melanie. He thought of them as rogue angels. When he came out of hospital, the summer was already over, but he'd never much liked the heat of the city in July or August; it was a close, deadly heat, a suffocation. He preferred the fall, with its lovely capitulations. Slowly, his original pain began to fade as well, and he was even capable of the occasional handshake, although the burning came back at times, for days or for weeks. It wasn't ever going to leave him. It was him, it was his. He gave up all his therapies, except for speech, and by Christmas of that year, when introducing himself to new people, he could say his own name again.

Letters to
My Grandma

Anusree Roy

This play is dedicated to Amma for starting it all,
Ma and Non for their strength and Baba for dreaming
his big dreams.

PLAYWRIGHT'S NOTE

Letters to My Grandma is a one-woman show. It is a play that focuses on
the life stories of two women, a granddaughter and a grandmother, and
weaves a journey through post-millennial Toronto to 1947 Burma, India.
Even though the play reads like a monologue addressing the audience,
it depends on stylized Indian dance movement. The transitions from one
character to another are created through movement or singing that allows
the audience to follow the narrative.

The dialogue mixes English, Bengali and Hindi, with the exception
of a Sanskrit mantra at the start of the play. The dialogue is spoken with
an "Indian Accent" and a "Canadian Accent."

CAST

MALOBEE AT 22	Granddaughter
MALOBEE AT 16	
MALOBEE AT 17	
GRANDMA AT 22	Grandmother
OLD GRANDMA	
GRANDMA AT 17	
GREAT GRANDMA	Great grandmother

LETTERS TO MY GRANDMA

MALOBEE AT 22 *takes position centre stage in an Indian dance pose. She is dressed in an Indian bridal sari. No specific jewelry to be worn. The stage represents various locations in India and Toronto at different times and years in the characters' lives. She is standing in present-day Toronto. She sings a Sanskrit mantra in praise of Lord Ramakrishna and performs a ritualistic dance.*

MALOBEE AT 22:

Om! Niram janam, nittam manam ta rumap. Bhakta nu kompa Dhrito bigh rohom boi, esha bo taram poromesh middam tangh Ramakrishnam shiresha namani.

(As MALOBEE AT 22 *says the following lines she puts a red dot on her forehead and eats a sweet.)*

Amma, today I am getting married are tumi nai.[1] You are not here. Kintu chinta koro na,[2] I brought all your letters with me. All of them. *(Pulls out a stack of letter from the folds of her sari.)* See, this is your last one, still unopened. *(Pauses and looks at the letter.)* I will. I will open it. It's just that I have been a...a bit busy with all the planning that I haven't had the time... *(Awkward pause. Searches for words.)* but dhako dhako...aami thik mone rekechie.[3] I still remembered it and brought it with me here. That's something, right? I am sure you have talked about how much you love me, how much you wish you were here, how much you are sad that...sad that...why I didn't...I will read it before... *(Pause. Breathes audibly for a brief moment.)* I thought of your hands all day today. I thought of us sitting in the car and I thought of you and I sitting and chatting for hours on end about Uttam Kumar and how much you wanted to learn how to write proper English. Jano to,[4] Amma, sometimes I think if we would have kept trying it would have happened. It really would have. You could have been able to talk to him in English. Remember that dream? The one of you and the Englishman talking in English while you laughed at his accent? That one. That could have

---

1. You are not here.
2. But don't worry...
3. Look, look...I kept it in my mind.
4. You know...

come true. Tumi probably bhabo[5] I gave up on you too soon. Na? Taki bhabo?[6] It doesn't matter... not that I can change it anyways. Onek din holo[7] since I last saw you, hopefully wherever you are, you are happy. There are so many people here today, to stand by me, to be with me. Ma, baba, Deepa, Shalini, Melanie have been up all night setting up the *huge* mandap. There are flowers all around the house. Downstairs, they are all sitting in a circle and singing for me. Kintu somehow kirokom lage, empty, phaka. Jano mone hoy,[8] if you were here I wouldn't need all of these people. I feel nervous, khoob khoob[9] nervous. If you were here...I would have asked you how all of this works. I am reading all these letters again and I am stunned by how much we have shared over the years...but there is such less truth in them; I get angry and think that they are filled with lies...filled with betrayal... you pretended to be happy there with your Muslim nurse and shared so much more with her than you wrote in these letters. I feel like time ran out on us, Amma. *(Takes a deep breath and pauses.)* Shabnam said that you kept asking for forgiveness...why? You are not the one who should be asking to be forgiven! What have you ever done that was so wrong? No, you know what, no. This is not fair; I want you to be here in Toronto with me when I get married. You told me...remember..."always always always"...so now? *(Takes a deep breath and gathers herself. Sits on the floor in front of the bridal plate.)* I am scared, jani na[10] if this is the right decision or not. You haven't seen him, that's why I doubt myself. Maybe I shouldn't. But then, now it feels like it is too late... *(Spots her grandma in the audience.)* Accha Amma,[11] how were you feeling when you were twenty-two and getting married?...seventeen! That's right, you got married to a man you had never met before. Then war. *(Picks up the bridal plate as she gradually stands up. Stares at the plate.)* You must have had one of these also. Right? Flowers, chandan, shidur, shak[12]...but I bet you didn't have an unopened letter. No... no you didn't. At twenty-two I am getting married and you were dealing with the aftermath of the war...

---

5. You probably think...

6. No? You think that?

7. It's been a while...

8. But, somehow it feels different, empty, so empty, it feels like...

9. Very, very...

10. I don't know...

11. By the way, Amma...

12. Sandalwood and other Indian bridal items that are on the plate.

(The plate suddenly drops from her hands, resulting in a sharp sound and scattering its contents. MALOBEE AT 22 *to* GRANDMA AT 22 *who speaks in a heavy Indian accent.)*

GRANDMA AT 22:

(Trying to hide herself while picking up a baby, she shouts.) Bachao... bachao....Kau ache...Aamar kache baby bachao[13]...shh...someone will come for us. Shh. Stay calm. Nothing will happen to you. Ma is here. *(She gradually stands up and starts walking while checking to see if her baby is alive.)* I walked miles after miles hoping that someone would recognize me. There was hatred in everyone's eyes. Everyone is dead...their eyes are dead. *(Notices a passerby.)* Dada, where is everybody? I have a baby only five hours old, dada, please help. Do you know where my family...No dada, we are Hindu. Our full blood is Hindu...not Muslim at all. What do you mean "Muslim trucks"? They don't have Hindu trucks picking up Hindu people? Why not? This is a Hindu area. Wait...wait...*(Notices someone else.)* Didi, my husband has left me...no...only a few hours old. Do you know where the Basu family is hiding? Which ship? When did they leave? What... listen...come back...No they didn't. They could not have left. We will find them, shona,[14] we will find them. You just stay alive...that's all you do. Ma will fix everything. Ma will be here. Always always always. Hai Thakur tumi dheko...tumi[15] *(Startled, turns around to the sound of a jeep roaring by.)* Eh wait wait! Please I have a baby...save us. Bhaisab...bhaisab, mai Muslim hoo.[16] I am a Muslim. Allah ki kasam.[17] I swear on our Allah. Ya mera baccha hai.[18] I just gave birth, bhaisab. Please bhaisab...you will be able to fit us all in your truck. No I won't. I will sit on the floor. If you want I will not even breathe in here. Look look...that woman that you have, she is not even Muslim. Allah ki kasam. She is the nurse that used to work in the women's ward. No she's not. The Hindus are taking up our space. She is not Muslim....See...Bhaisab wouldn't you carry a Muslim and her child so Allah blesses you? My family is very rich, you take me to the ship and my husband will give you money.

---

13. Save me! Save me! Is anyone here? I have a baby!

14. Sweetheart...

15. Dear God, you see us through, you...

16. Brother...brother, I am Muslim. ("Brother" is a term of respect used to address a stranger.)

17. I swear on Allah.

18. This is my child.

Get the nurse off! Get her off!

You are Hindu. What baby?...see these Hindus will come and make up stories. I don't know her. Allah ki kasam. Please bhaisab we are wasting time. The ship will leave soon and I have to find my husband so he can give you money. *(Pushes the nurse off the jeep and gets on. The jeep roars away.)* Thank you Sree Ramakrishna, thank you Sree Ramakrishna, thank you Sree Ramakrishna, thank you Sree Ramakrishna, jai Thakur, jai Thakur, jai Thakur, jai Thakur, jai Thakur, Allah, Allah, Allah, Allah, Allah, Allah...

(Long pause. GRANDMA AT 22 *looks around the jeep. Speaks in a low whisper.)* Are you all Muslim? Me neither. Will you pray with me for her? She was the Muslim nurse, Najma, who helped me deliver my baby. *(Closes her eyes and prays.)*

(GRANDMA AT 22 *transitions to* MALOBEE AT 16, *a new immigrant who has just arrived with her parents at Pearson International Airport in Toronto.)*

MALOBEE AT 16:

Ma, you will not even believe, they have something called "automatic flush." You just stand there and it flushes!

We are waiting for baba to come back. Why does it have to rain? Stupid rain. Ruins everything, I thought our first day in Toronto would be...I don't know...bright and sunny. Oh, baba is coming.

Ki holo?[19]...What do you mean he didn't answer his phone?...Will immigration be able to help us?...Wait, I'll come. *(Follows her father to the immigration counter.)* I am fine thank you, and how are you? Good. Umm... I was wondering if you could please help us. We just came in the BA 99 flight and...hmm? No BA 99 from Calcutta, to Heathrow to Toronto. Yes. No. No complaints. They were very nice. Yes, they gave us lunch and peanuts. *(Awkward.)* Thank you...yes. We have our luggage. Yes, the problem is that we have been waiting, for a very long time now. Yes outside and it's raining. Umm...no...we don't have relatives...but Malkit Singh, from the immigration company, was going to pick us up...WWICS...oh World Wide Immigration Consultancy Service. We will stay at their guest house

---

19. What happened?

for a month. Can you give him a call for us?...Yes, my father tried but he is not answering...maybe if you call...please ma'am we are new in Toronto. Oh, sorry...anyone else can help? Oh...okay. Good night to you too.

(MALOBEE AT 16 *and family leave the airport.*) Ummm nake maye...shahajo korte parche na...uff...ki ousgho![20] Baba, I think we should just take a taxi... do you have the address? Also, can we buy a phone card to call Amma? (MALOBEE AT 16 *walks upstage to enter guest house. Looks astonished.*) Ehhh baba! Why are we sharing this room? Ma? Didn't baba book this? Then... why do we have to share? If we paid the full money we should have the full room. Aren't there any other rooms in this guest house? Uff! I can't share one bed! Uff...let's just go back to India. *(Frustrated, sits on the floor. After a pause, looks up startled by someone calling her name.)* Ha? I have the phone card...I'll call. *(Looks at the phone card and dials a number, then pauses.)* 416-883-8335 *(Pause.)* English. *(Pause.)* One. *(Pause.)* What does press pound mean? *(Pause. Dials the international number, then pauses.)* 011-91-33-24722190 *(Pause.)* Ah! Ringing. Hello. Is this Briddho Old Home? I am calling long distance from Canada...can you connect me to room 14C...yes 14C...Yes, quickly please. *(Pause.)* Hello, Amma. Tumi kamon aacho?[21] Yes we have reached Canada safely...no it was on time. There were no problems at all. Ha, he came to pick us...it is very beautiful here... ha, no they are very friendly. Yes...I like it...Yes, a lot. Tumi kamon aacho? How is your Nurse Shabnam doing? Ah ha...don't worry Amma, you will like her soon. Give it some time. Hmm...did you take Autrin today?... Good...Okay, talk to baba and I will talk to you again...

(Scene shifts to MALOBEE AT 16 *standing in the bus line with her father and mother. She is very conscious of the way other people are standing and is subtly trying to copy them, and is practising her Canadian accent. She speaks in an Indian accent.)*

MALOBEE AT 16:

Cooool, wooorrddd, peeecee, props, I would totally do her. *(Startled by the arrival of the bus. Gets on and addresses the driver.)* Good morning to you also. Sorry...I am a new here. Is it two dollars? Oh okay. Sorry, my mother, father and I need to go to a mall called Zeelers mall to buy jackets. Could

---

20. Ummm, annoying woman. Couldn't she help us...uff...how irritating!
21. How are you?

you tell us when that comes...The people in the guest house where we are staying said its near Sheerway Gardens Mall. Oh sorry. We thought like American. Sorry. Zellers.

(To her father.) Arre, baba,[22] move in. Don't hold the line no. Sorry we new here. Baba, you go sit down and I'll talk to him. *(To the driver.)* Oh thank you kindly sir. What is this? What is a transfer mean? Like a receipt? See... because we are new...so we...oh yes yes. I said that already. No it's okay, I don't need a receipt...I pay fare no? *(Listens intently to the driver.)* Oh aacha aacha.[23] I see. I will just quickly explain to my father. Okay...you drive... but please call for Zeelers stop. Thank you. *(Calls out to her father.)* Ek bar fare ta dele...so aamara jokhon[24] will get on train, we don't have to pay again. If we show the receipt we can get in for free. *(To the driver.)* Ha...that is a really good system no? Free train rides with receipt. I have to write this to my grandma. She will find this receipt business funny. *(Walks to her seat looking intently at the transfer. Then looks out the window.)* Oh, baba, dhako dhako![25] Such huge trucks...they look like trains from Calcutta. Look. I think like fourteen to sixteen wheels no? See, driver, I was telling my father... the trucks that we see are like so long they are like trains in my country. We have small trucks like lorries. They are small like a bus here. Everything is big big here and so clean. Only little newspaper on the bus. There though, so much dirt. Everywhere. Also, you know how here, the driver can stop the bus and go to the Teem Hottoon Place, Aare that place selling coffee, okay Hortens. Yes, as I am saying, you know how you can go to Teem Hortens and buy coffee in the middle of driving the bus, in my country if you get off even to go toilet somebody will steal your bus and drive away. Haa...no lies. The thiefing is not that much there...but still I can totally see that happening. Or they might be so angry that you have caappaacino and they are sweating so much in the heat that they will burn the bus. No, really. I am telling the truth. Why you laughing? Another thing in my country, fare is so much cheaper, Two dollars is like sixty rupees. You can buy one plate meal with that. But we don't get receipts on the bus...We are buying jackets from Zeelers today because winter is coming soon...Oh sorry. *(Pause.)* This is our stop? Sorry, bye bye. Bye bye. Oh okay back door. Excuse me. Oh thank you kindly. Have a nice day and thank you again.

---

22. Oh dad...
23. I see, I see.
24. So once we pay the fare, so when we...
25. Oh, dad, look, look!

(MALOBEE AT 16 *transitions to* MALOBEE AT 17 *sitting on the floor writing a letter.*)

MALOBEE AT 17:

Sricharaneshu Amma, bhalo accho?[26] *(Looks up at the audience.)* Dear Amma, how are you? Got your letter last week. That took quite a while, ha? Three weeks since you posted it. *(Gets up.)* Anyway, Kichu bolar aage boli,[27] I am sorry. I don't think I can end up going to India. I don't have enough money this year. I tried, Amma, I really did, kintu jete parbo na. Khoob khoob khara lagche, Amma, Kintu[28] I really have no choice. I swear as soon as school ends I will go and be with you. Nothing in the world will get in the way. Promise. Promise. Promise. There, I said it three times. I hope you are taking your Autrin daily, please do not forget it and don't overdose. Bhalo laglo[29] talking to you last night, but there was no time to tell you a lot. Today is the thirteenth, one full year in this new country, ha? Ki tara tari time flies na? Bishashi ei hoy na[30] it was just last year that I wrote to you saying how much I hated the winter in Toronto. But now I can't wait for it to snow. It looks so beautiful outside. You can see the beautiful patterns of the flakes. This year ma has given me really warm gloves. Last year er moton are thanda lagbe na. Ek bochore koto ta profoundly change kore gachi! Eai mone hoy kalekai[31] we landed in the airport, cold and wet from the rain, somehow managing to sleep all four of us on that one bed and now one full year has somehow passed jani na kotha theke.[32] I still feel new, still like an immigrant. I am not sure when or how that will change but I know that for now it is still there. Even in small things, aamar mone hoy,[33] that I am not totally fitting in. In everything there has to be a fitting in. Rocker, punk-er, rave-er, pop-per...all of them have their own fitting in groups at the caf. Caf mane[34]...like lunch room. School here is so different, Girls and *boys* are

---

26. Respected Amma, are you well?
27. Before I say anything, let me say...
28. I tried, Amma, I really did, but I cannot go. I feel really, really bad, Amma. But...
29. It was nice...
30. How quickly time flies, no? I cannot even believe that...
31. I don't feel as cold as last year. Things have changed so profoundly in one year!
   It feels like yesterday...
32. I don't know from where.
33. I think so...
34. Caf meaning...

allowed to wear any coloured nail polish and big big earrings. Can you imagine, if Mrs. Gulati saw this in Our Lady Queen of the Mission she would send me right down to the main office. *(Laughs.)* Also, they don't call it "tiffin time" here; they call it "lunch break." Deepa and I have fries and pop for one dollar when we have some extra money. Pop meaning like Pepsi or Coca-Cola, like cold drinks...cold drinks. Anyways, I have a teacher here, Mrs. Hardy. She is Indian, married a white man. It is totally acceptable here. Whites marry blacks, and Indian marries Chinese, probably cows marry chickens! They still make fun of me though, calling me Paki, so I guess they are not that accepting, but I am used to it. Don't worry at all— the people who call me that are not my friends anyways. I think the next time someone calls me that I will call them an "American" and then they will get my point. Oh, and also what's really funny is that they think Hindu is a language and Hindi is a religion.

Anyways, Mrs. Hardy gave us an assignment for OAC English class. I have to write about the most influential person in my life and of course I picked you. I feel like we spent our entire lives together, without really getting into detail. I have so many questions for you. Why didn't you tell me more about the war? Ma tells me these stories that you have *never* told me about. I don't even know what to ask you. What was it like to be on a train with refugees? *(Sits on the floor.)* Ma said that Japan used to carpet bomb Burma? And you had to steal from other people to eat? How did you feel when Dadai came back four years after the war? When you thought he was dead and they made you wear widow's white? Why didn't you hate him for that? Actually come to think of it, did you ever truly love him? He was twelve years older, what were you thinking? Why didn't you say something? To your parents, to me? All these years I have lived with you and now that I have moved far I am trying to get to know you. *(Pause.)*

There is a lot of getting to know going on right now...there is a British boy...he is nice. He is my friend Helen's older brother. His name is Mark. Mark Castleman. I am getting to know him too. Oh and Amma, don't worry I say my mantra that you taught me all the time.

(MALOBEE AT 17 *transitions into* OLD GRANDMA. OLD GRANDMA, *who has difficulty walking along with a shaky right hand. She speaks in a heavy Indian Accent.)*

OLD GRANDMA:

I am happy to know that you say your mantra. Do not ever forget it. I hope
you have gotten a good jacket from that Zeellers mall this year also. It
will keep you warm. Make sure to wear your scarf and gloves. Your letter
made me cry and made me laugh for so many reasons. You have asked so
many questions to me for this class. Not sure where to start...whatever
you do, don't tell all the white people I studied until grade eight only, they
might think I am foolish. Jani na kano kono dino tomake kichu bole ne
kano.[35] I guess I thought that you had better things to do. Sometimes I wish
I had gotten to learn that English from you. Remember that Englishman
dream...to make that come true. Khob shok chilo[36] to learn English and
sing in English...Just like the Englishmen did in the war. Tumi hoyto
bhabte je aami[37] selfish...taking up all your time. I didn't mean to, just
wanted to talk to you like your friends. Jai hok, aar purono diner kotha bole
lab nai.[38] You asked about the war. War, the bloody messy war. *(Transforms
to GRANDMA AT 17.)*

Yes, I was seventeen when my father married me away. From wealth to
middle class, I never argued. At seventeen had my first baby; he left me the
day before the delivery. Shorge gachen tai ninda korbo na.[39] He went to a
town called Shwebo to build dams on rivers, I never argued. After what felt
like years of starvation and hiding, the war ended. I came back to India
from Burma with my little baby, and sat with the refugees on the ship. They
touched me—I was a wealthy man's daughter—but I never for once argued.
Monomoy came back four years later, I gave birth again and he got a job
in Burma. Burma, the land that I swore I would never go back to. I packed
my bags and never argued. Civil war broke out in Burma, and once again we
fled. We fled, leaving everything. The beautiful house, cabinets filled with
china...and my beloved jewelry. All that baba had given to me was buried
with so much money. But I made sure I saved my bangles for you. I thought
I could come back one day and....*(Sees her dead husband Monomoy appear
and addresses him.)* Monomoy, you came back after four years. Did you
ever think of me? They made me wear widow's white...did you know that?

---

35. I don't know why I never told you anything.

36. I had a deep desire to...

37. You must have thought that I am selfish...

38. In any case, there is no point talking about those days...

39. He has gone to heaven so I won't criticize him.

Don't walk away while I am talking to you. Why didn't you write to me? Did you not care if it was a boy or a girl? She was our first...*(Transforms back to* OLD GRANDMA.*)* ha Malobee I eventually loved him. Of course I did. Why wouldn't I? He was a strong and loving father to my children. I loved him till the day he died. When I was seventeen, my ma said, "Aamra tomar jonno khoob bhalo bor dhekeche. Baba hai bole deyeche and you are getting married in May 5ᵗʰ." I said, "How can I get married? I have not even seen him once, ma, and May 5ᵗʰ is only three months away." Ma said: "Ummmm...to ki? Tin mash! Shob arrangement hoy jabe. Tui shudu aamake bol tui Naker ring na Naker stud chas? Oh aah!!! Aami bhabchie fish chop, dal makani, chicke butter masala, cutlet, big big breasts of chicken, tandori aar rice shudo starter hobe. Also, Aar baba ke bole debo jano gulab jamun aanen? Tui Bol. Naker ring na Naker stud?"

(OLD GRANDMA *transitions to* GRANDMA AT 17. *She is accompanied by* GREAT GRANDMA *who is a funny character with big exaggerated hand movements and speaks primarily in Bengali.*)

GRANDMA AT 17:

(To GREAT GRANDMA.*)* I don't know...my nose is not even pierced. Hmm... may be a hoop. Make sure it is big and round with little bells hanging. Not too many, just three little bells. Oh also, can I have a red veil with gold stars on it? *(Pauses.)*

GREAT GRANDMA:

Ummm...shudo stars kano chai. Aami toke moon aar stars kore debo. Bhari Gold deye. He is an engineer. Thakur aamar parthona shunechen. Tomake kintu bhadro hote hobe. Prochur Dowery chaiche, kini, chinta korish na...shob think hoye jabe.

GRANDMA AT 17:

(Pauses for a long while.) Kintu ma,⁴⁰ if he is an engineer he should have money no? How will you pay that much dowry? And what if he doesn't like me? Can I see him once? Only one glimpse. Please ma...please...

---

40. But ma...

GREAT GRANDMA:

Ki ulto palta kotha bolcho aamar shamne? "Not like" mane ki re? Bhalo na lagar ki aache? Aamader khob bhalo mai. Ekata meye bol to je passes class eight? No even one! Ha! Aar shono. Beye bhalo laga aar na lagar neye tomake chinta korte hobe na ... shudo compromise koro aare shob this thakbe. Aar ekabar complain korle, aami tomake chor marko Tumi seventeen years old...too old. Tommar baki shob bhondu ra have been married arr ekahon aar having children. Uff...kobe je tumi grow up korbe! *(Gives* GRANDMA AT 17 *a pair of bangles.)*

Eai nao. Aamar mother aamake deyechelo jakhon aami married hocchilam. Tomar jonno rekechilam. tumi safe rekho...

GRANDMA AT 17:

Oh ma. Na. Oh! Ma go, thank you. Ami eta ke chiro kal treasure kore rakhbo. Tomar oto shoker jinish[41]...Thank you ma. I will pass them on. I promise, promise, promise.

*(*GRANDMA AT 17 *transitions to* MALOBEE AT 22 *who is speaking on a cordless phone at her house in Toronto.)*

MALOBEE AT 22:

Hello...hello...na na, Amma, listen to me. Your letter arrived yesterday. Thank you. Thank you so much. I will write back as soon as I get a minute, actually my third-year exams are on. So I am a little bit busy.

Anyways, listen, Amma, How many times did you take the Autrin? *(Pause.)* What? Na, you have to only take it once. Once a day, like you always have. *(Pause.)* Hello? Yesterday Nurse Shabnam said that you fell in the bathroom? *(Pause.)* No Amma, she doesn't lie. You have to be very careful, Amma, when you go. Pa tep tep jeyo,[42] and always bring a towel with you. Nurse Shabnam is very nice, Amma; tell her to make sure that you don't lock the door okay? Hello? Could you please put Nurse Shabnam on the phone. I promise that I will talk to you as soon as I am done with her. I promise,

---

41. I will forever treasure this. These are your beloved...
42. Press your feet to the ground while you walk...

promise, promise. You wait right there. Of course, I have to talk to you. Wait there okay? Ebar Nurse Shabnam ke debe?[43] The nurse. No not Mary, Shabnam! Hello? Amma? *(The line has gone dead.)* Ami arr pani na![44] *(Puts the phone down and starts to write a letter.)* Hello, Mrs. Shabnam. Thank you. Thank you for taking such good care of my Amma. There are a few things I want to go over. I hope you got the cheque that baba sent you. Could you please mail me the receipts? I know you know all of this, but I am just making sure. Autrin has to be taken once a day. Make sure she doesn't lock the door. Give her a clean towel as well. *(Pause.)* I will not be able to come down this year either. *(Pause.)* It's been challenging. Mrs. Shabnam, I don't mean to be demanding, but I have a favour to ask. If there is some money left over from the grocery cheque, can you please buy Amma some jub jubs? Make sure there are lots of orange ones and put them in a clear plastic bag and leave it near her pillow. Thank you very much. Sincerely Malobee Basu. *(Looks at letter, shakes her head and puts it down. Starts to write another letter.)*

Srichoronashu Amma. Ki holo?[45] Dear Amma, what happened? You hung up the phone again on me! I hope everything is alright. I have something I want to tell you…I wanted to ask you on the phone. *(Long pause.)*

Anyways, Mark asked me to marry him and I said yes. I know that means that I am not coming this year, but I told him we have to go to India for the honeymoon. I can see you, you can see him and he can see India. So, in another year, at this time I will be there with you. So sorry Amma. You have to believe me, I am doing this for a reason. Amma, bahable ki rokom lage.[46] You and me again. We can go and sit in the Victoria Memorial Hall and have orange jub jubs. Start making a list of things that you want to do. A year will fly by in no time. Aaj ekhane shesh korchi. Nejer khal rekho.[47] Love you. Tomar aadorer[48] Malobee.

(MALOBEE AT 22 *transitions to* OLD GRANDMA, *who speaks in a heavy Indian accent.)*

43. Now can you give [the phone to] Nurse Shabnam.
44. I can't deal with this anymore!
45. Respected Amma, what happened?
46. When I think about it, it feels so strange.
47. I am stopping here now. Take care of yourself.
48. Your beloved…

OLD GRANDMA:

Nurse? Nurse? Shabnam? Shabnam? *(Pause.)* She has decided to marry the British boy. *(Long pause.)*

What you are saying? How is that good? A British boy with British parents and grandparents. I am sure they all eat beef.

They all must sit at their British tables with their rotten teeth while eating British food and talk about British people and British life. Nurse? Where are you? Wait on a minute. Please sit on the floor for one minute. *(Pause.)*

How much does she know about their family? How much does she know about their lifestyle. Their past? Who are they? Does he know who we are?

No Nurse...I don't need the bedpan cleaned. You just listen to me. Give me two minutes, Nurse...just listen to me.

Oh kono dino jante parlo na,[49] Nurse. Never never never. Aamari mork-homi[50]...why so many years I never shared anything? Why so many years I kept it all in like a closed book! Dying for someone to read me.

I want you to get the paper and pen from the table and write what I am about to say. Write my Malobee this letter.

Look Nurse look. Dhako, nejer...nejer chok deys dhakho,[51] Shabnam. Look Shabnam. Look at my sari. Look at me sitting on the ground. I am so young. Still wearing white. I didn't know that my beloved husband was alive. I didn't know that he would walk for a month and see my parents. I didn't know that he would wait for me without marrying again and we would make love again.

Look at me sitting there. See the pain in my eyes. I am clutching to that baby whose umbilical cord is completely infected, I didn't know that this baby would grow up to be a beautiful daughter and she would give birth to you, Malobee.

---

49. She never knew...
50. My stupidity...
51. Look, look with your own eyes...

Look Nurse. One year has passed I am in a town called Ochin.

(OLD GRANDMA *transforms into* GRANDMA AT 17.)

GRANDMA AT 17:

Today is one full week of this bombing from Japan! What is this happening Bhai?[52] Why are they not telling us anything? How many more days will we be in hiding? They think they can come anytime and they will place a few bombs and we have to be okay with it. The British go and Japan come... we didn't say anything and now that Japan is helping us...British back. Are pari na.[53]

Bhai, I am going to the shed. I will take out some food from hiding... Ration is low here...do you hear me? I will be in the shed...please make sure no one comes!

(GRANDMA AT 17 *goes to the shed and starts looking through shelves. Startled by a noise, she looks up. British soldiers have burst into the house next door looking for women.*)

(*In a whisper.*) Jai Ramakrishna, Jai Ramakrishna, Jai Ramakrishna, Jai Ramakrishna, Jai Ramakrishna. Hai Thakur aamake bachao. Thakur. Khoma kore dao.[54] Please, please. (*Standing, crosses her legs slowly and places one hand over her right thigh to protect herself.*) Please God. I have come this far...don't take this away from me. I will give the British everything...but not this. This is for my husband, God. He will find me. Save me oh Rama Krishna. Please. God, make sure they don't take this away from me... (*British soldiers can be heard leaving the house.*) Thank you Thakur thank you Thakur. (*Cries and collapses on the floor.*)

(*Light changes indicate time change.* GRANDMA AT 17 *transitions into* MALOBEE AT 22 *who is holding the letter.*)

---

52. Brother.

53. I can't do this anymore.

54. Hail Lord Ramakrishan [repeated]. Dear God, please save me. Dear God, please forgive me.

MALOBEE AT 22:

(Throws the letter down and runs off stage. Vomiting sounds can be heard.)

*(*MALOBEE AT 22 *transitions to* OLD GRANDMA *sitting and rocking back and forth.)*

OLD GRANDMA:

Nurse? Oh Nurse? Come sit beside me...just this once. Come. *(Long pause.)* Will you touch my face? *(Closes her eyes and responds to the nurse's touch, placing one hand on top of the "nurse's hand" on her cheek.)* I am so happy that you are here now. Are you that Shabnam that I threw off that jeep? Yes...yes you are...Why have you not come to see me before? I waited for you all these years. I have begged Allah to save your life. Will you forgive me? Ha? Will you forgive me? I was greedy. I wanted to save my baby....Forgive me for throwing you from that jeep. I...I want to thank you for staying with me that day...but you had so much hate in your eyes. Everyone had left me when I arrived at that hospital...but you stayed on....I have nothing to give you now...but here take these. You can have all my jub jubs. *(Holds out a handful of jub jubs and drops them. They scatter on the floor.)* See, I give you all...even the orange ones...just you let me go of this pain I have carried for so many years. Forgive me please, Shabnam. *(Long pause.)*

Nurse Shabnam...you are writing this, right?...Write this...Malobee, I am happy that you are marrying. Good. British people are good. I think. Not so good at the war time though...but now maybe are good. Write: I am happy that you are marrying...write it again. I am taking my Autrin, daily. Daily, I am taking my Autrin daily. *(Pulls out the bangles that* GREAT GRANDMA *had given her.)* When I buried everything, when everything got buried in their soil, I saved these. For the future, for you, my love. I somehow knew. These bangles will be there with you when I can't forever be with you. I love you my beloved shona moni. I took my Autrin today. *(Pause.)*

*(*OLD GRANDMA *transitions to* MALOBEE AT 22, *wearing her bridal sari and stands, as at the top of the show, with an unopened letter in her hand.)*

MALOBEE AT 22:

(Stares into the audience.) I wanted to tell you that...I will remember this journey with you. The road beyond is for me to discover...but I know... and I know this because I truly believe it that you will be travelling with me. I think...the truth is that I was the one that betrayed you...I was the one that didn't come. I was the one that couldn't open this last letter for so long. It has been sitting on the table as I stared at it. Why? How could I? How could you? How could you write a letter to me and decide on your own that this will be the last one? After so many letters that we have sent back and forth...suddenly this is the last one? How could you not have waited for me, Amma? Was it planned? Is your absence from my wedding your revenge on me? On baba and ma for moving away...so many miles away? Remember, you told us to move on. Remember you told me to go find myself. And now I have. I really have. But I miss you in me. I miss you here, with me. I didn't open this letter...because I knew I would have to forgive. Myself. *(Pause.)* For not being there for you. I know what it feels like now...to be lonely even with so many people around you. *(Pause.)* In your own way...you are here. Tumi kosto kore gach na bhalo bhabe gacho...aami kono dino jane parbo na...kintu aami etta jani je...ami tomake bhalo bashi..[55] *(Rips open the envelope and pulls out the bangles.)* Thank you for sending me the bangles... I am going now...with you with me...

(The End.)

---

55. I am not sure if you died in pain or peace, but I know this much...I love you very much.

CONTRIBUTORS

JUDY FONG BATES is the author of *Midnight at the Dragon Café* and *China Dog and Other Stories*. In 2006 *Midnight at the Dragon Café* was the winner of an Alex Award from the American Library Association and was named an ALA Notable Book. *Midnight at the Dragon Café* was the featured book in February 2007 for the One Community Reads Program in Portland, Oregon. She divides her time between Toronto and Campbellford, Ontario. At present she is working on a family memoir.

SAMANTHA BERNSTEIN recently completed her MA at York University, where she researched youth movements, epistolary literature and the politics of subjectivity; part of the thesis was an autobiographical epistolary novel about social activism among the children of North American baby boomers. She has also recently completed a poetry manuscript, *Industrial Evolution*. Her work has appeared in *Exile, Books in Canada, YorkU Magazine, Studio* and *The Fiddlehead*.

LORELI C. BUENAVENTURA grew up writing, directing and performing in popular theatre, and was a newspaper columnist in Winnipeg's Filipino community. She was co-founder and arts editor of the former national literary magazine, *Pagitica in Toronto*. Her works have appeared in the United States and Canada, including on CBC Radio. She is also a seasoned communications professional who draws from her multidisciplinary background in the arts, finance, and community and international development. She is currently the manager of The Mentoring Partnership, a program of the Toronto Region Immigrant Employment Council.

SHILA DESAI comes from a family of multigenerational immigrants. Her grandparents and parents emigrated from India to Kenya to Britain and then Canada. Desai was born in Kenya and she knew early on that she too would move around the world, taking her patchwork of memories in each culture to form the basis of her writing. Although she has been writing stories since grade school for friends' reading pleasure, "The Tangerine Conundrum" is her first published short story. She lives in Thornhill, from where she has a perfect vantage point into Toronto's multicultural montage, and feels little urge to move again—with the world down the street.

STACEY MAY FOWLES has been published in various online and print magazines, including *Kiss Machine, Girlistic, Absinthe Literary Review* and *subTERRAIN*. Her non-fiction has been anthologized in the widely acclaimed *Nobody Passes: Rejecting the Rules of Gender and Conformity and First Person Queer*. Her first novel, *Be Good,* was published with Tightrope Books in November 2007, and her next book, *Fear of Fighting,* will be released with Invisible Publishing in fall 2008. She lives in Toronto where she is the publisher of *Shameless Magazine*.

JAMES HARBECK is an editor, mainly. He is the first person in his family to be born in Canada; previous generations trace back through the eastern United States to before the revolution. He grew up in the Bow Valley in Alberta, got his PhD in theatre at Tufts University, near Boston, and now lives in deep downtown Toronto. He sings in the Toronto Mendelssohn Choir and runs. He is currently trying to find a home for his book of salacious verse about English usage.

WASELA HIYATE was raised in Toronto and has lived in Europe, Asia and the Caribbean, working as everything from waitress to television producer. "Mo" is from a collection of short stories about travel, cultural alienation and globalization. Wasela holds a MFA from the University of British Columbia's Creative Writing Department. Her work has appeared in the *Malahat Review, Grain* and *Descant* and is forthcoming in *The Land and How It Lay,* an anthology by Invisible Publishing. She is currently researching exotic travel destinations as a means of escape from the task of writing a novel.

CLARA HO writes poetry, prose and everything in between and has performed at various venues across Toronto. When she is able to find the time, she writes as much as she can about how human beings relate or don't relate to one another.

BARBARA HUNT is a dry-eyed nostalgic who delivers contemporary bites of naked truth wrapped in a rich appealing texture. She writes poetry, fiction and non-fiction from her home in Port Perry, Ontario, where she regularly contributes to a local monthly magazine, *Focus on Scugog*. Her work has been published by CBC Radio One, *The Globe and Mail*, *Metroland*, *Esteem* and *Homemakers Magazine* as well as several anthologies. She can be reached at <www.writersplayground.ca>.

SAYEEDA JAIGIRDAR was born in the leafy tea-garden district of Sylhet, Bangladesh, and grew up on three continents as she travelled with her father, who was a diplomat. She was educated in England, Sweden, India and Bangladesh. After completing her MA, she was a lecturer in English at Dhaka University for some years. Jaigirdar immigrated to Canada in 1998 and now lives, writes and teaches in Toronto. Her writing explores the relationship between time, space and character. She received the Toronto Arts Council Award for Emerging Writers 2007 for her novel-in-progress, *The Song of the Jamdanee Sari*. Jaigirdar is working on the novel with her mentor MG Vassanji through the Humber School for Writers.

AISHA SASHA JOHN is a Vancouver-raised writer and dancer living in Toronto. Her work has appeared in *Exile Quarterly*, *Contemporary Verse 2*, *ACTA Victoriana* and *Carousel*. She is currently in her first year of the University of Guelph's Master of Fine Arts in Creative Writing program. Aisha is working on a short story collection and a poetry manuscript entitled "Citizen of Heart."

ELPIDA MORFETAS is a teacher and writer who was born in Athens and grew up in Toronto. Her work also appears in the creative non-fiction anthology *Our Grandmothers, Ourselves: Reflections of Canadian Women*, and is based on her grandmother and the experience of immigrating to Canada with her in the early 1970s. Elpida has studied at the University of Toronto and Carleton University in Ottawa. She has taught English, literature and history in Greece and at various Toronto high schools and colleges. She continues to write and teach in Toronto.

MOLLY PEACOCK, poetry editor of the *Literary Review of Canada*, has written six volumes of poetry, including *The Second Blush* and *Cornucopia* (W.W. Norton). She is the general editor of *The Best Canadian Poems in English. Paradise.* She has published a memoir, *Piece by Piece*, as well as *How To Read a Poem and Start a Poetry Circle* by McClelland and Stewart. Peacock's one-woman show in poems, *The Shimmering Verge*, toured North America, including an off-Broadway showcase.

MICHAEL REDHILL is a poet, playwright and novelist. His most recent publication is the novel *Consolation*, which was long-listed for the 2007 Man Booker Prize. He is currently living in France.

MONICA ROSAS is an educator/agitator/artist whose work aims to challenge and provoke discussion on gender, the environment and the visible minority experience. A second-generation Colombian Peruvian Canadian she was born and raised in a boisterous blue-collar family in Ontario's one and only city of steel, Hamilton. She has since lived and worked in Colombia, Cuba, Peru and Venezuela teaching English and drama. Currently, she is an English and social science high school educator who works with at-risk youth in Toronto.

ANUSREE ROY recently completed her MA at the Graduate Centre for the Study of Drama at the University of Toronto. Her recent theatre credits include playwright and performer of "Pyaasa" in 2007 at Theatre Passe Muraille, playwright and performer of "Letters to My Grandma" at Diaspora Dialogue's Keep Toronto Reading in 2008, and assistant director for "No Exit" and "The Times" at York University and for "Straight as a Line" for Summer Works at Factory Theatre. She also performed a solo piece titled "breathlessness" for Tarragon Theatre's 2006 Spring Arts Fair and for Diaspora Dialogues at Hart House at the University of Toronto in January 2007. Anusree completed her internship at Nightwood Theatre's Ground-swell Festival last year and is currently writing "Brothel #9," a new play that explores the sex-working industry in Calcutta.

ALISSA YORK is an acclaimed novelist and short story writer whose recent novel, *Effigy* (Random House Canada), was shortlisted for the 2007 Scotiabank Giller Prize. She has lived all over Canada and now makes her home in Toronto, where she is currently at work on her third novel. To learn more, go to <www.alissayork.com>.

Keli Maksud was born in post-colonial Kenya and moved to Toronto
to complete her education. Her practice deals primarily with the ongoing
discourse about cultural appropriation, authenticity—identity.

About the cover image:
"It is essential for me to give a sense of my own background as it is the
basis of my practice. I studied at a private school taught in English; however,
my native tongue is Swahili. Growing up, we listened to Michael Jackson
and MC Hammer; we watched American, South American and Kenyan
programs. One could say that my generation is more rooted in the MTV
culture than in our own Kenyan culture, which is being drained of its own
authenticity. This is a reality that manifests itself with diverse cultures all
over the planet. My own sense of culture and identity has evolved from
a hybrid of cultures that are present here. Simultaneously there has been
unconscious pressure for me to fit into a cultural stereotype (African)
and to produce work that falls easily into this projection. This has led me
to question different ideas of a fixed identity belonging to an "authentic"
culture or place. My interests have centred on African textiles, i.e., their
use and the historical relationship that they have with the West. I find it
effortless to use collage as my methodology as it speaks of my own hybrid
experience. I combine images from fashion magazines, old photographs
taken in colonial Africa, and fabrics bought in Toronto and Kenya so as to
question or perhaps challenge various notions of authenticity both in art
and identity."

Diaspora
Dialogues

Diaspora Dialogues supports the creation and presentation of
new fiction, poetry and drama that reflect the complexity
of Toronto back to Torontonians through the eyes of its richly
diverse writers.

For information on our publishing and mentoring programs,
or on our monthly multidisciplinary performance series,
please visit www.diasporadialogues.com or call 416 944 1101.

Diaspora Dialogues gratefully acknowledges the support of
The Maytree Foundation, Ontario Trillium Foundation,
Heritage Canada and the Government of Canada through the
Book Publishing Industry Development Program.